STECK-VAUGHN/BERRENT

THE Long Island Story

GLORIA SESSO
REGINA T. WHITE

STECK-VAUGHN
BERRENT
PUBLICATIONS

About the Authors

Gloria Sesso is currently a teacher and supervisor of social studies for Half Hollow Hills School District in Dix Hills, New York. She is the president of the Organization of History Teachers and a former president of the Long Island Council for the Social Studies.

Dr. Regina T. White is currently principal of Buckley Middle School and director of curriculum of Rhinebeck Central Schools in Rhinebeck, New York.

Credits

Design and Layout/Cover Design: **Jan Jarvis/Michael William Printery**
Cover Photo: **Peter Paul Muller**

Reviewers

Doreen A. Andersen
Nesconset Elementary School
Smithtown School District
Smithtown, New York

Arnold Mason
Social Studies Coordinator
South Manor School District
Manorville, New York

Maureen Ann F. Fallon, Ed.D.
Director of Social Studies and
Language Arts
North Babylon School District
Babylon, New York

STECK-VAUGHN
BERRENT
PUBLICATIONS

The Long Island Story

ISBN # 0-8172-6383-7

Published by Steck-Vaughn/Berrent Publications, a division of Steck-Vaughn Publishing Corporation.

8 9 10 073 07 06 05

Contents

UNIT 1 Geography

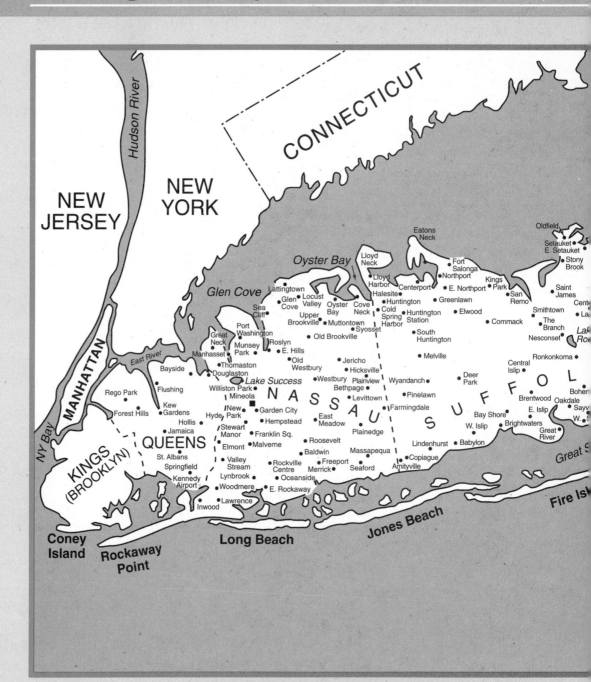

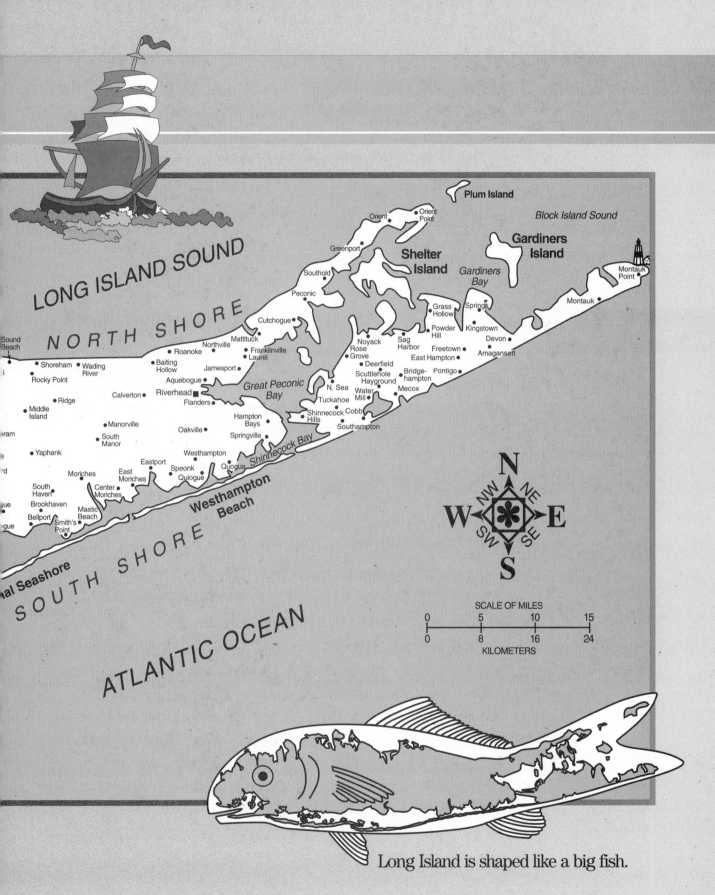

LONG ISLAND SOUND

NORTH SHORE

Plum Island

Block Island Sound

Orient
Orient Point

Greenport

Shelter Island

Gardiners Island

Southold

Gardiners Bay

Peconic

Montauk Point

Cutchogue

Grass Hollow
Springs

Montauk

Sound Beach

Mattituck
Northville

Noyack
Rose
Grove

Sag Harbor

Powder Hill

Kingstown

Devon

Roanoke

Franklinville
Laurel

Freetown

Shoreham
Wading River

Baiting Hollow

Jamesport

Deerfield

East Hampton

Amagansett

Rocky Point

Scuttlehole
Hayground

Bridge-hampton

Pontigo

Aquebogue

Great Peconic Bay

N. Sea

Mecox

Ridge

Calverton

Riverhead

Tuckahoe

Water Mill

Flanders

Middle Island

ram

Manorville

Oakville

Hampton Bays

Shinnecock Hills
Cobb

Springville

Southampton

Yaphank

South Manor

Westhampton

rd

Moriches

Eastport

Speonk

Quogue

Shinnecock Bay

East Moriches

Quiogue

South Haven

Center Moriches

Westhampton Beach

Brookhaven

gue

Bellport

Mastic Beach

Smith's Point

nal Seashore

SOUTH SHORE

ATLANTIC OCEAN

N
NW NE
W E
SW SE
S

SCALE OF MILES

0   5   10   15
0   8   16   24
KILOMETERS

Long Island is shaped like a big fish.

CHAPTER 1

A Tour of Long Island

Before You Read

How much do you know about the place where you live? This chapter will help you to answer questions about the location and size of Long Island. Do you think Long Island is a nice place to live? Why?

NEW TERMS

- geography
- island
- South Shore
- barrier beach
- bay
- shoreline
- sand dunes
- North Shore
- cliff
- cove
- harbor
- Long Island Sound

*W*hat if someone asked you where Long Island is located? Would you be able to answer?

Let's take an imaginary airplane ride over Long Island. This will give you a clearer picture of Long Island's *geography*. To prepare for this trip, study the map on pages 2 and 3.

Your private airplane

The Shape of Long Island

Long Island is part of New York State. It is one of the largest islands in the United States. An *island* is a body of land surrounded on all sides by water.

Can you see why Long Island is called "Long Island"? The island is much longer than it is wide. It is 118 miles in length from New York Bay to Montauk Point. Its widest point is between Lloyd Neck and Seaford. That distance is 20 miles.

Study the shape of Long Island. What does it remind you of? Long Island looks like a great big fish. The head of this fish is near New York City. The tail or fins end at Montauk and Orient Points.

From head to tail, this fish is made up of four counties. They are Kings (Brooklyn), Queens, Nassau, and Suffolk.

A narrow body of water separates Long Island from New York City. It is called the East River. At one end of the river, the end by Nassau County, is the Long Island Sound. The New York Bay is at the other end of the river, by Brooklyn.

Looking east across Long Island

Where is the South Shore?

The South Shore

Are you ready to begin your trip? Your plane will travel from the head of the fish to its tail. This means the plane will fly from west to east. On the return trip, it will fly from east to west.

Your plane takes off from John F. Kennedy International Airport in Queens. You find yourself high above the *South Shore*. The water to the south, or to your right, is the Atlantic Ocean. Notice the narrow strips of land in the water. They separate the mainland of Long Island from the Atlantic Ocean. These land strips are called *barrier beaches*.

In between the barrier beaches and the mainland are bays. A *bay* is a body of water connected to an ocean and partly enclosed by land.

The land along the sea is called a *shoreline*. The southern shoreline of Long Island is always changing. On the beach, the wind blows the sand into small hills called *sand dunes*. Over

Sand dunes

What role does Long Island's climate play in the formation of sand dunes?

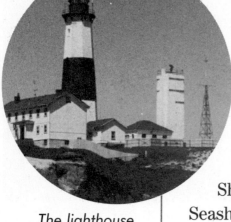

The lighthouse at Montauk Point

What function does a lighthouse serve?

time, sand dunes may grow, move, or even disappear due to the action of the wind. Waves wash sand away from one beach and deposit it elsewhere along the shoreline.

Your plane passes many beach areas. Soon, you are above the tail of the fish. You can clearly see the beautiful lighthouse at Montauk Point. When the lighthouse was first built in 1795, it was 297 feet away from the ocean. The shoreline has changed. Now the lighthouse is almost at the water's edge.

There is another famous lighthouse on the South Shore. It is the one at the Fire Island National Seashore. Made in 1859 of brick and cement, the lighthouse's tower is 168 feet tall. This lighthouse, one of the tallest when it was built, was used to direct traffic between New York and Europe. The Fire Island lighthouse

The Fire Island lighthouse

Why is the tower of a lighthouse painted with bold designs?

A marina in Port Jefferson on Long Island Sound

Why would Port Jefferson have a marina?

is still used today. Its wide black and white bands make it easy to see.

If you climb to the top of either lighthouse on a clear day, you will get a great view of Long Island.

The North Shore

So far, you have been flying along the South Shore. Now your plane crosses the island and turns west. You will fly west along the *North Shore* for your return trip. The northern side of the island is very different from the southern side. The South Shore is flat and sandy. The North Shore is hilly and rocky. The South Shore stretches almost in a straight line. The North Shore has many curves.

High, steep rocks, called *cliffs*, rise sharply from the northern shoreline. There are also many bays and coves along the North Shore. A *cove* is a small bay surrounded by hills. Many coves are used for harbors. A *harbor* is a

A closer look at the North Shore

How can you tell that this is a photo of the North Shore?

protected body of water where ships can anchor. Coves make good harbors because the hills around them protect them from wind and waves.

The North Shore is bordered by a long stretch of water. It is called the *Long Island Sound*. A *sound* is a long body of water that connects two larger bodies of water. The Long Island Sound connects the East River and the Atlantic Ocean. It is about 20 miles wide and more than 100 miles long.

Finally, your plane returns to Kennedy Airport. You are at the end of your trip. You should now have a clearer picture of the island you live on.

Recalling What You Read

Use the words in dark print to finish each sentence.
Write the words you choose in the correct blanks.

dunes   **North Shore**   **barrier beach**   **South Shore**   **island**

1. A body of land surrounded by water is a(n) _____.

2. Hills and rocks are found on the _____.

3. Hills of sand formed by the wind are called _____.

4. A narrow strip of land that separates the mainland from the ocean is a(n)

   _____.

5. Flat and sandy ground is found on the _____.

Think About It

1. Explain why you think that "Long Island" is or is not a good name for Long Island.

   _____

   _____

   _____

2. The Montauk lighthouse is now at the water's edge. When it was first built in 1795 it was 297 feet away from the water. Why do you think that is so?

   _____

   _____

   _____

Problem Solver

The barrier beaches of Long Island are in great danger. Working in small groups, have each group investigate the problems of one of the barrier beaches. Do the following:

1. Describe the problems of the barrier beaches. Draw a diagram or picture to demonstrate what has been happening.

_____

_____

2. Explain what has been done to help solve the problem.

_____

_____

_____

3. Suggest your own solution to the problem and tell why you think it would work.

_____

_____

_____

Map Builder 1

What Is a Map?

A map is a flat drawing of the Earth or parts of it. A map can show a city or a state or even an island. Maps show things you can see like mountains, rivers, and roads. They also show things you can't see like boundaries between states. How do you read a map? Here are some things you need to know.

Title
This explains what the map is all about.

Compass Rose
This shows you how to find directions. North, south, east, and west are the four main directions. It also gives halfway directions such as northeast (NE).

Symbols
These are signs or pictures that have special meanings. Symbols can take the place of words.

Map Key
All symbols on a map are grouped together in the map key, or *legend*. The legend tells what kind of information is on the map.

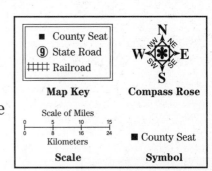

Scale
This explains how distances on a map relate to the actual distances. For example, an inch on a map may stand for ten miles.

Below is a map of Long Island. Look at the map, then answer the questions below.

1. Tell why it is necessary to have a map key.

_____

_____

2. What problems could occur if a map did not have a compass rose?

_____

_____

CHAPTER 2

Landforms and Climate

Before You Read

This chapter will explain why the North and South Shores are different and how this difference came about. What do you think caused the differences outlined in Chapter 1?

NEW TERMS

- glacier
- Ice Age
- peninsula
- erosion
- neck
- climate
- current
- Gulf Stream
- topsoil

*Y*ou now know that the North and South Shores are very different. The North Shore is hilly and rocky. The South Shore is sandy and flat. What caused these differences? One reason is glaciers. Thousands of years ago, Long Island was shaped by glaciers.

The Formation of Glaciers

A *glacier* is a large mass of ice. It can be hundreds of feet long. It can be several miles wide. It is formed when a large amount of snow falls and doesn't melt.

A modern-day Canadian glacier

What were the effects of glaciers on Long Island's landscape?

The snow packs together into a giant sheet of ice. The ice sheet becomes too heavy. It then moves slowly toward the sea.

You will no longer find glaciers in most parts of the world. It's not cold enough. Thousands and thousands of years ago, it was very cold. This period of time is called the *Ice Age*. Here's what the Ice Age did to Long Island.

Giant glaciers covered most of North America. As they melted, they left rocks and sand and gravel. They made flat plains on the South Shore. They left rocky hills on the North Shore. They carved out large holes. Two of these are Lake Ronkonkoma and Lake Success.

The peninsula at Montauk Point

Why is the lighthouse there?

The Formation of Peninsulas

Another difference between the North and South Shores is the shape of the shoreline. Waves constantly beating on the rocky North Shore caused the formation of many peninsulas.

A *peninsula* is a piece of land that sticks out into the water. It is like an island. There is one important difference. A peninsula is surrounded by water on only three sides.

Some peninsulas are formed by waves crashing against the shore. The rocky land won't move. The soft soil around

13

it washes out to sea. This leaves a peninsula. This washing away of the soil is called *erosion*.

Early settlers thought that some of these peninsulas looked like *necks*. There are towns on Long Island with the word neck in their names. Remember the fish-like shape of Long Island? The fish's tail is really two peninsulas.

Beach erosion at work

What can be done to prevent this from happening?

The Climate of Long Island

The ocean also influences Long Island's climate. A *climate* is the kind of weather a place has over a period of time. Long Island has a mild climate. This means it is not very hot or cold.

In the winter, the temperature rarely drops below 10 degrees Fahrenheit. In the summer, it usually stays below 90 degrees.

Fishing in the Atlantic Ocean

What are some of the advantages of living near the ocean?

You learned that Long Island is surrounded by water. This keeps it cool in the summer and mild in the winter. In the summer, breezes from the water cool the land. The summer sun warms the water. The water then stays warm. This helps keep the temperature mild in the winter.

There is a warm *current* of water that flows through the Atlantic Ocean. It is called the *Gulf Stream*. It flows northeast out of the Gulf of Mexico. The Gulf Stream helps warm the breezes that blow over Long Island. It keeps the winter from being too cold.

Mild winters make Long Island a popular place to live and farm. The climate is very helpful to farmers. It gives them a longer growing season. The island receives an average of 43 inches of rain a year.

Long Island's sandy soil is not always helpful to farmers. They must add lots of fertilizer to improve the topsoil. *Topsoil* is the top layer of earth. It is darker than the soil under it. Plants need a good topsoil to grow in.

Unloading potatoes

What would a farmer like about working on Long Island?
What would he/she like to change?

By now, you know that Long Island's appearance is always changing. This is because the ocean, wind, and people are constantly at work.

Recalling What You Read

Draw a line from the term to the words that best describe it.

1. glacier   a. first layer of earth

2. neck   b. type of weather

3. topsoil   c. a peninsula

4. climate   d. huge ice sheet

Think About It

1. Write a geographic description of Long Island that would persuade a person to live there.

_____

_____

_____

_____

_____

_____

2. Turn to the map on pages 2 and 3 and find all the towns or villages that have the word "neck" in their name. Why do you think they were named that way?

_____

_____

_____

_____

_____

Problem Solver

Keep a daily record of the temperature where you live on Long Island. Read the weather report in the newspaper or watch the weather report on television and record the temperature each day. Keep this record for at least ten days. At the end of the ten days plot these temperatures on a graph.

1. Write a statement to describe what the graph shows.

   _____

   _____

   _____

   _____

2. Explain why the graph came out the way it did.

   _____

   _____

   _____

   _____

Map Builder

Reading a Map

Map Builder 1 explained some things you need to know about maps. You learned about the compass rose and symbols. You found out what a map key and scale are for. This lesson will give you practice in reading a map.

Do you know how to use the map key? Let's find out. First, locate each of the symbols contained in the map key on the map below. Start with the county seat of Suffolk. With a pencil, trace an imaginary journey by interstate highway to the county seat of Nassau.

From the county seat of Nassau, go south to the intersection of the nearest state road pictured on the map. Use the compass rose to help you with the direction. Finally, proceed west on the state road, crossing over the county boundaries of Queens and Kings (Brooklyn).

Now you can see how a map key not only gives us information, but helps us get where we want to go.

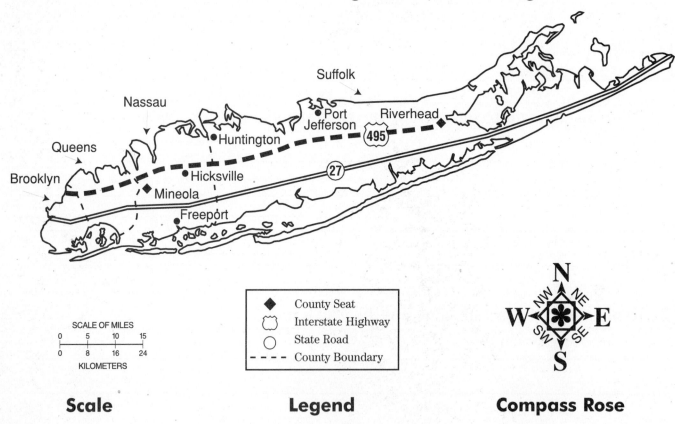

◆	County Seat
⬡	Interstate Highway
◯	State Road
- - -	County Boundary

SCALE OF MILES

0	5	10	15
0	8	16	24

KILOMETERS

Scale   **Legend**   **Compass Rose**

Using the map on page 18, complete the following questions.

1. You want to go from Freeport to Port Jefferson. What direction would you travel?

   _____ .

2. According to the map scale, 20 miles is approximately how many kilometers?

   _____ .

3. Which road is an interstate highway? _____ .

4. The county seat of Nassau is _____ .

5. If you wanted to know how many miles you were going to travel from one place to another by car, how would you measure the miles and why?

   _____

   _____

   _____

   _____

   _____

   _____

True and False

If the underlined word makes the sentence true, write "true" on the line to the left. If the underlined word makes the sentence false, write the correct word on the line to the left.

_____ **1.** Long Island is shaped like a <u>fish</u>.

_____ **2.** Long Island is 118 miles long from New York to <u>Bayport</u>.

_____ **3.** The body of water that separates New York City from Long Island is the <u>Great South Bay</u>.

_____ **4.** A <u>bay</u> is a body of water that connects to an ocean and is partially enclosed by land.

_____ **5.** The South Shore of Long Island is <u>hilly</u>.

_____ **6.** <u>Glaciers</u> helped to shape Long Island.

_____ **7.** Long Island has a <u>short</u> growing season.

_____ **8.** The Gulf Stream makes Long Island <u>colder</u> in the winter.

_____ **9.** Long Island is made up of <u>two</u> counties.

_____ **10.** Long Island has a <u>mild</u> climate.

LI Inquiry

1. Water has both good and bad effects on Long Island's geography. Explain why this statement is true.

   _____

   _____

   _____

2. Explain why the climate of Long Island is desirable.

   _____

   _____

   _____

Exploring Long Island

Project 1

Make a Map of Long Island

With your class, make a large papier-mâché or salt and flour map of Long Island on a piece of board.

Paint the geographic features of Long Island and label them. Also paint and label the water bodies surrounding Long Island on the board.

As you continue your studies of Long Island, additional features can be added — roads, towns, historic places — so that when you have finished your study of Long Island the class will have a large, complete map of Long Island to display.

Early History

This circa 1880 painting by Edward Lamson Henry is called "Beach Wagon." It shows a descendant of the Algonquians proceeding through the countryside.

CHAPTER 3 — The Algonquians

Before You Read

The Algonquians were the first people to live on Long Island. Many people believe that it is incorrect to call the Algonquians "Indians." Instead they think we should call them Native Americans or American Indians. Why do you think this is so?

NEW TERMS

- Algonquians
- family group
- wigwam
- dugout canoe
- preserve
- sign language
- Great Spirit
- manitous

*L*ong Island is full of towns with names like Setauket (se TAW ket) and Montauk (MON talk). These are Algonquian (al GONG kin) names. The *Algonquians* were the first people to live on Long Island.

Dutch and English settlers came to Long Island in the early 1600s. Long before these settlers arrived, as many as 6,000 Algonquians inhabited the island.

Family Groups

These Native Americans lived together in large *family groups*. There were more than a dozen of these groups on Long Island. Each group or band had its own name. They named themselves after the place where they lived. The Long Island Algonquians were part of a larger group of Algonquians that lived along the eastern coast of North America.

An Algonquian

How can you tell that he is an Algonquian?

24

Clothing

The Algonquians did not wear large feather headpieces. They might place one or two feathers in their hair. On special days, the Algonquians painted their faces and bodies. They made this paint from plants, clay, and powdered stone.

Men dressed in deerskin pants, called *leggings*. They also wore animal-skin cloaks. To keep cool in the summer, they wore very few clothes.

The Algonquian women braided their long, dark hair. Married women had one braid. Unmarried women had two. The men shaved off most of their hair and left only a two-inch-wide strip. This strip was in the middle of the head.

The women wore deerskin skirts all year-round. They decorated themselves with jewelry made from seashells. Both the men and the women wore slipperlike moccasins on their feet.

A wigwam

What are the people doing inside the wigwam?

Homes

What was it like for Algonquian children on Long Island? Try to imagine yourself in the following lifestyle. Children lived with their families in dome-shaped huts called *wigwams*. These were made from tree branches, bark, and dry grass.

A hut was built by placing tree branches in a circle around bent tree limbs. There were two doors covered with animal skins.

Inside furnishings were simple. Animal-skin mats were placed on the floor. Algonquians slept on wooden benches covered with animal skins. In the middle of the wigwam was a pit for the fire. This was where the Algonquians cooked their food. A hole in the roof let the smoke out.

Wigwams were built in groups or villages. Usually, a village was near a good supply of fresh water. The Algonquians also tried to settle near open fields. This made farming easier.

A hunter

What do you think he is hunting?

What did the Algonquian children have to eat? There was plenty of meat and fish on Long Island. The meat came from deer, bears, ducks, and turkeys. Clams, oysters, and fish were popular, too. Vegetables, such as squash and corn, were an important part of meals. Nuts and berries were served often.

Growing Up in an Algonquian Village

Algonquian children spent most of their day helping the adults gather and prepare food. Older boys went with their fathers to learn how to hunt and fish. They used bows and arrows to kill birds and other animals. They also carried spears and clubs with stone heads.

The Algonquians used the same types of fishing tools that we use today. They fashioned their lines from animal or plant fibers. Their hooks and sinkers were made of stone, wood, or bone. Some caught fish in large nets.

Hunting was done in a group. The boys helped their fathers make the hunting tools. They also gathered building supplies. They would cut young trees with stone axes. They would collect reeds, grass, bark, and animal skins. They hollowed out trees by burning or scraping to build *dugout canoes*.

Algonquian girls helped their mothers with cooking and farming. To prepare for winter, they

Catching fish

How are these men catching fish?

Daily chores

What are some of the daily chores that you see being done in the picture?

26

preserved meat. Meat was preserved by smoking it over a fire or drying it in the sun. It was then stored in a large trench or ditch. Some vegetables were dried in the sun.

Algonquian women and girls made their own clay pots for cooking. They wound long coils of clay together. Then, they shaped and smoothed these coils into pots.

The girls often had to take care of the younger children. They would carry a baby strapped to their backs on a long, flat board. The girls also helped their mothers build wigwams.

Algonquian children did not go to school as you do. Their lessons were learning how to do the jobs of the adults. If they wanted to go somewhere, they had to walk or take a canoe.

Most family groups had their own spoken language. They also communicated through *sign language* and drawing pictures. In sign language, hand symbols are substituted for a word or group of words.

Building a dugout canoe

Why do you think it was called a dugout canoe?

Did the children ever have time for fun? Like you, they played many games. The boys pretended that they were great hunters or warriors. The girls enjoyed a game like the hopscotch children play now.

Religion

Dancing was popular among the Algonquians. They danced in a group. They told stories through their dances. Sometimes the dances were part of a religious ceremony. The dances were created to please the *spirits*.

The Algonquians believed in spirits whom they called manitous. They believed the spirits were in nature. They believed they could be good or evil. They believed that in a good mood, the spirits taught them how to build houses, grow corn, and start cooking fires. In a bad mood, the spirits made terrible storms or played tricks on hunters so that they missed their kill.

A Native American dance

Why might they be dancing?

Recalling What You Read
Use the terms in dark print to finish each sentence.
Write the terms you choose in the correct blanks.

sign language   **wigwams**   **Algonquians**   **school**   **dances**

1. Algonquian children did not go to _____.

2. The Algonquians lived in dome-shaped huts called _____.

3. Family groups sometimes communicated through _____.

4. The Native Americans of Long Island are also called _____.

5. The Algonquians told stories through their _____.

Think About It

1. Explain what you would have liked best about being an Algonquian child.

_____

_____

_____

_____

2. What would you *not* have liked about Algonquian life? Explain.

_____

_____

_____

_____

Problem Solver

Adriaen Van der Donck wrote A *Description of the New Netherlands* in 1655. In it he described what he had seen of Algonquian culture. One thing he noticed about the Algonquians was that they believed that the rivers, the woods, and the plains were open to all groups to use, if they didn't quarrel or harm the land.

1. How is this belief related to the belief in manitous? Do you think the following connection can be made? Why or why not?

    Belief in manitous .... shows a respect for nature

    _____

    _____

    _____

    _____

2. What other parts of Algonquian life could be connected to the belief in manitous? Why?

    _____

    _____

    _____

    _____

Map Builder

Outline Map

Study the outline map of Long Island. Look over the list of places. Match up the numbers to the places in the blanks below.

Long Island Sound _____   Montauk Point _____   a barrier beach _____

Atlantic Ocean _____   North Shore _____   East River _____

a peninsula _____   a bay _____   South Shore _____

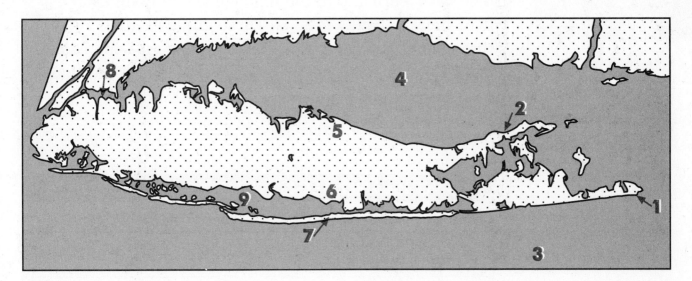

Ask your teacher to help you find a map of your community. Your local school district or telephone book may have one. Use this map as a model. In your notebook, draw your own outline map of your community.

Show the boundaries of your local area. Put a compass rose on the map and begin your key. Start with symbols for your school and home. Place them on the map. You will keep adding to this map as you study Long Island.

Do you like classroom projects? Begin a big map of your community for the classroom. Get some other students to help you.

Algonquian Families

CHAPTER 4

Before You Read

In this chapter, you will learn how the Algonquians governed themselves. Is it important for a society to have leaders? Think of the many different ways in which leaders help a society.

You have learned that the Algonquians of Long Island lived in large family groups. These groups settled throughout the island. Each family group on Long Island had its own name. These names described how the Native Americans saw the areas in which they lived.

NEW TERMS

- Sachem
- Wyandanch
- Tackapausha
- Sunsquaw
- wampum
- seawan
- Paumanok
- reservation

LONG ISLAND ALGONQUIAN FAMILY GROUPS	
Name of Family Group	**What It Means**
Canarsie (ka NAR see)	the fenced place
Rockaway (ROCK a way)	sandy place
Merrick (MARE rick)	at the barren land
Massapequa (mass a PEE kwa)	great water land
Secatoag (SEK a tawg)	black or dark-colored land
Unkechaug (UNK e chawg) or Patchoag (PAT chawg)	land beyond the hill
Shinnecock (SHIN ni cock)	flat or level country
Montauk (MON talk)	fort country
Manhasset (man HAS set)	neighborhood
Corchaug (KOR chawg)	the greatest place
Setauket (se TAW ket)	land at the mouth of the river
Nissequogue (NISS a kwag)	the clay or mud country
Matinecock (ma TINE cock)	at the hilly land

The Meaning of Algonquian Names

The family group living in the Babylon area called themselves the Secatoag (SEK a tawg). The meaning of the Native American word *Secatoag* is "black or dark-colored land."

On the previous page is a chart of the names of the Long Island Algonquian family groups. Read each name, using the letters in parentheses to help with pronunciation. Check its meaning.

Now let's see where these family groups lived. Study the map below. It matches up the locations of the family groups with some present-day geographic locations.

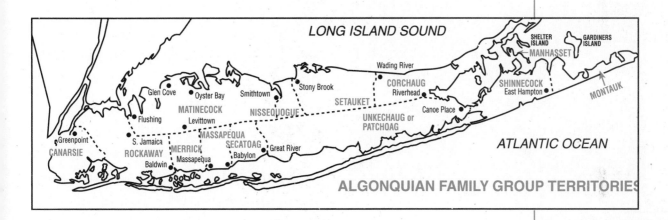

LONG ISLAND SOUND

SHELTER ISLAND GARDINERS ISLAND

MANHASSET

Wading River

CORCHAUG
Riverhead

SHINNECOCK
East Hampton

MONTAUK

Glen Cove Oyster Bay Smithtown Stony Brook

SETAUKET

Canoe Place

MATINECOCK NISSEQUOGUE

Flushing Levittown

UNKECHAUG or
PATCHOAG

ATLANTIC OCEAN

Greenpoint

CANARSIE

S. Jamaica
ROCKAWAY MERRICK
Baldwin Massapequa

MASSAPEQUA

SECATOAG Great River
Babylon

ALGONQUIAN FAMILY GROUP TERRITORIES

The Sachem

Each family group had important people. These important people were called *Sachem* (SAY chem).

In the early 1600s, one of the great chiefs of Eastern Long Island was called *Wyandanch* (WY an danch). He was a Sachem of the Montauks. The Montauks were good fighters. They protected their land against enemies. Other Algonquian families on Eastern Long Island needed this protection. They feared attack by the warlike Native Americans who lived across Long Island Sound.

Stephen Pharoah, a Montauk, lived until 1879.

What were the Montauks like?

A Sachem

How do you know that this is an important man?

Another Sachem of the early 1600s was *Tackapausha* (tack a PAW sha). He was head of the Massapequa on western Long Island.

Tackapausha signed many peace treaties between the Native Americans and European settlers. In Seaford, there is a wildlife preserve named for him.

What were the official duties of Sachems? They settled arguments between families in his village. They also settled arguments between his village and other villages. He was expected to lead his people in time of war.

Sometimes, the Sachem was a woman. She was called a *Sunksquaw*.

Some of the women who became Sunksquaws were the wives or widows of Sachems. Others became a Sunksquaw on their own.

The Importance of Wampum

To show he was important, a Sachem sometimes wore strings of *wampum*. Wampum comes from a Native American word meaning "string of shells." It was also called *seawan*.

Wampum was made by cutting clam or conch shells into small pieces. Then holes were drilled through these pieces. The next step was to string them into necklaces or belts.

Families used wampum for trading with one another. The Long Island wampum was greatly valued. Neighboring Native Americans were ready to fight to gain this valuable wampum.

To keep peace, the Algonquians of Long Island often gave wampum to stronger Native American groups from New England. This was called "paying tribute." The Long Island Algonquians called their island *Paumanok*, or "land of tribute." They may have chosen that name because they paid a high price to live there.

The Beginning of Reservations

Very few Native Americans are left on Long Island. Many died from smallpox, a disease brought by the white settlers. The land of the Native Americans was taken over by the Dutch and English colonists. Many of the remaining Native Americans moved to new areas where they hoped to live undisturbed.

Some of the Native Americans who stayed on Long Island were moved onto *reservations*. A reservation is an area of land set aside by the government. Two small reservations still exist on Long Island. One is the Poosepatuck (POOS pa tuck) Reservation in Mastic. The other is the Shinnecock Reservation in Southampton.

Native Americans played an important role in Long Island's history. What reminders of the Native American way of life can you find in your community?

Recalling What You Read

Draw a circle around the word that best completes each sentence.

1. The leader of a family group was called a _____.

        Shinnecock   Sachem   settler

2. A great chief of Eastern Long Island was _____.

        Tackapausha   Paumanok   Wyandanch

3. The Native Americans named Long Island _____.

        Paumanok   Montauk   Setauket

4. The Algonquians traded strings of shells called_____.

        reservations   leggings   wampum

Think About It

1. Explain the difference between a Grand Sachem and a Sachem. Tell how the duties of a Sachem are similar to or different from government leaders today.

_____

_____

_____

_____

2. The Algonquian "paid tribute" to live on Long Island. Explain what you think would have happened if they did not pay tribute.

_____

_____

_____

Problem Solver

In 1768, Charles Wolley wrote a journal. In it, he described Native American lives on Long Island. He wrote about how valuable wampum was. He noticed that when an Algonquian male wanted to get married he "asks the consent of the Parents...he gives her so many Fathom of Wampum according to his ability."

1. Why do you think the Algonquian man gave the woman wampum to become his wife?

_____

_____

_____

_____

_____

_____

2. What does this tell you about the importance of women in Algonquian society?

_____

_____

_____

_____

_____

Map Builder

The Algonquians

Study the map below. The Long Island Algonquian family groups have been numbered according to where they lived. Using the map on page 33, match up the numbers to the family groups in the blanks below.

Shinnecock _____   Nissequogue _____

Canarsie _____   Merrick _____

Rockaway _____   Secatoag _____

Matinecock _____   Setauket _____

Montauk _____   Massapequa _____

Unkechaug _____   Manhasset _____

Corchaug _____

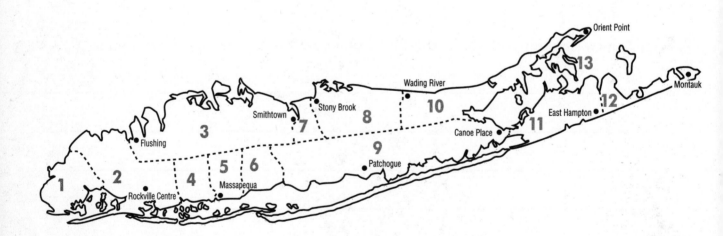

Using the map on page 38, complete the following questions.

1. Which places on the map are named for the Algonquian families?

   _____

   _____

   Are they near where the family for which they are named lived? _____

2. Why do you think so many places on Long Island are named for Algonquians?

   _____

   _____

   _____

   _____

   _____

3. Choose a family group from the chart of family names and what they mean on page 32. Then turn to the map on page 38 and find out where that family lived. What do you think that place is like, based on the meaning of the family name?

   _____

   _____

   _____

   _____

Before You Read

In this chapter, you will learn about how surprised the Native Americans were when Dutch traders sailed into New York Bay. Can you think of the reasons why they might be surprised?

NEW TERMS

- Henry Hudson
- Dutch East India Company
- John Cabot
- Giovanni da Verrazano
- Adrian Block
- New Amsterdam
- Lange Eylandt
- Dutch West India Company
- Peter Stuyvesant

*F*or the Native Americans of Long Island, transportation was simple. They either walked or went by canoe. Imagine their surprise when *Henry Hudson* sailed the Half Moon into New York Bay on September 4, 1609. They had never seen a large ship before.

Captain Henry Hudson

What do you think he is wearing around his neck?

The Discovery of Long Island

Captain Hudson was an English explorer. He was working for the *Dutch East India Company* of Holland. Holland was a country in Europe. Today it is called the Netherlands. Its people are called the Dutch. Check the map on this page to see where Holland (the Netherlands) is located.

The Dutch East India Company was an important trading company. It was run by rich businessmen in Holland. This company asked Hudson to find a shorter route from Europe to Asia. Instead, he found Long Island.

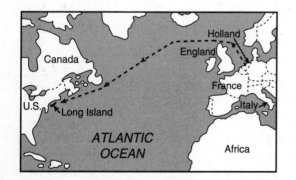

Hudson and his crew first went ashore on what is now called Coney Island. Check the map to the right. You will see that Coney Island is part of Brooklyn.

Was Hudson the first explorer to visit Long Island? No one knows for sure. The English, or British, claimed that *John Cabot* came first. Cabot is supposed to have traveled along the South Shore in 1498. He did not come ashore.

Others say *Giovanni da Verrazano* was first. In 1524, Verrazano sailed into New York Bay. Verrazano was an Italian explorer who worked for France. He sailed along the eastern coast of the New World. He did not make a map or immediately report his discovery.

In 1964, a newly built bridge was named after him. On this map, you will see that the Verrazano-Narrows Bridge joins Long Island with Staten Island.

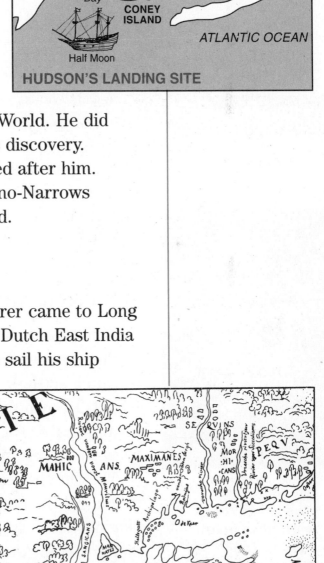

The Exploration of Long Island

Five years after Hudson, another explorer came to Long Island. *Adrian Block* also worked for the Dutch East India Company. It is believed he was the first to sail his ship completely around Long Island.

Block drew a rough map that showed Long Island was an island. The map is pictured here. How is this map different from a modern one? In honor of Block, an island was named after him. Block Island is at the eastern end of Long Island.

After the explorations of Hudson and Block, the Dutch claimed Long Island. They were already familiar with the island we call Manhattan.

First map of Long Island

A Dutch household

What are the activities going on in this room?

They had built trading posts and a small fort there. They named Manhattan *New Amsterdam* after Amsterdam, an important city in Holland. The Dutch gave Long Island its name by calling it *Lange Eylandt.*

Settlement and Trade

A new company, the *Dutch West India Company*, was formed to keep control over Long Island. It offered land to Dutch settlers who would start farms on western Long Island. To own this property, settlers had to farm the land for ten years. They also had to give one-tenth of what they grew to the company.

The Dutch West India Company was powerful. It tried to control the colonists by appointing strict governors. One of these was *Peter Stuyvesant*. He acted like a dictator. A dictator is a leader who uses power unfairly. Stuyvesant would not give the colonists religious freedom.

The Dutch West India Company wanted the colonists to trade only with their products. This made the people angry. Many colonists refused to follow the company's orders.

Peter Stuyvesant, governor of New Amsterdam from 1647 to 1664

Does he look like the man you have been reading about? Why or why not?

Why was Long Island so important to the Dutch West India Company? The Dutch wanted to gain control of the Long Island wampum, the strings of shells the Algonquians used for trading. They traded the wampum with Native Americans from other areas. This was the way the company got valuable animal skins. Those skins could then be sold in Europe for a nice profit.

The Long Island Algonquians were eager to trade with the Dutch settlers. They wanted the inexpensive cloth the Dutch brought from Europe.

The Dutch trade with the Native Americans.

What do you think they are trading?

The Contributions of the Dutch

The Dutch people made many contributions to Long Island. They introduced many holiday customs. Children looked forward to St. Nicholas Eve and Day. The Dutch children believed that St. Nicholas came riding over the rooftops on a white horse. He would leave presents for the good children in their wooden shoes. The bad children found hay and sticks. Later, St. Nicholas became known as Santa Claus.

Easter was another special holiday for the Dutch. On Easter Sunday, they ate boiled eggs. These eggs were colored with dyes from the bark of trees.

Dutch houses had special features. A long slanting roof came down over an open porch. The doors were in two sections. There was a top and a bottom. Each could be opened separately.

The Dutch introduced sports like ice skating and bowling. They brought tulip bulbs from Holland. What Dutch influences have you noticed on Long Island?

A Dutch Colonial style house

What are some special features that you can see?

Recalling What You Read

On the blank lines, write the name that best identifies each statement.

1. _ _ _ _ _ _ _ _ _ _ _   The first explorer to sail around Long Island.

2. _ _ _ _ _ _ _ _ _ _ _ _   An English explorer who was the captain of the Half Moon.

3. _ _ _ _ _ _ _ _ _ _ _ _ _ _ _ _ _   A group of rich businessmen who wanted a shorter route to Asia.

4. _ _ _ _ _ _ _ _ _ _ _ _ _ _ _ _ _ _   An Italian explorer who sailed into New York Bay.

5. _ _ _ _ _ _ _ _ _   An English explorer who sailed along the South Shore.

6. _ _ _ _ _ _ _ _ _ _ _ _   An island named for the explorer who circled Long Island.

7. _ _ _ _ _ _ _ _ _ _ _ _   The Dutch name for Long Island.

8. _ _ _ _ _ _ _ _ _ _ _ _ _ _   A Dutch governor on Long Island.

9. _ _ _ _ _ _ _ _ _ _ _ _ _   The area of Long Island where Hudson came ashore.

10. _ _ _ _ _ _ _ _ _ _ _ _   The name of the Dutch settlement on Manhattan Island.

Think About It

1. Why do you think the rich businessmen in Holland asked Henry Hudson to find a shorter route from Europe to Asia?

   _____

   _____

   _____

   _____

   _____

   _____

2. Tell why you think it was or was not fair for the Dutch West India Company to want the colonists to trade only with them.

   _____

   _____

   _____

   _____

   _____

   _____

Problem Solver

Quakers were a religious group that tried to settle on Long Island during Dutch rule in 1657. Peter Stuyvesant tried to stop them. Some people that already lived on Long Island did not agree with Stuyvesant. They thought the Quakers should be allowed to live on Long Island. They made this famous statement to Stuyvesant. Read the statement and think about the questions that follow.

"We cannot stretch out our hands against them...We desire therefore in this case not to judge lest we be judged...let every man stand and fall to his own Master...We are bound by the law to do good unto all men, especially to those of the household of faith...Therefore if any of these said persons come in love unto us, we cannot in conscience lay violent hands upon them...for we are bound by the law of God and man to do good unto all men and evil to no man...."

1. What do you think this statement means? Which words do you think are most important? Why?

_____

_____

_____

_____

_____

_____

_____

_____

_____

Map Builder

The First Map of Long Island

Adrian Block was an explorer who worked for the Dutch East India Company. In 1614, he drew what is believed to be the first map of Long Island, along with the area around it.

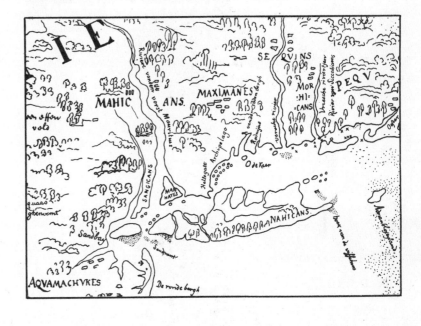

1. Can you recognize any of the words written on Block's map? What do you think words like "Morhicans" and "Manhates" mean?

_____

_____

_____

_____

_____

_____

_____

2. Using adhesive notes or small slips of paper, write your own labels for this map, pointing out modern place names and boundaries.

CHAPTER 6

English Colonists

Before You Read

The English were also interested in settling Long Island. The Dutch lived mostly in Brooklyn and the English moved into the eastern end of the island. Why do you think the English moved so far away from the Dutch?

NEW TERMS

- charter
- King Charles II
- Colonel Richard Nicolls
- saltbox houses

*D*uring the early 1600s, more English than Dutch came to Long Island. These early English settlers came from other colonies in New England. They came for religious freedom. They wanted to own land that their children could inherit. They believed Long Island could offer them a better life.

English Settlement of Long Island

Some English families lived in Dutch communities. The Dutch West India Company allowed English people to buy land from them. Government leaders were afraid the English and Dutch would not get along.

In 1650, these leaders met in Hartford, Connecticut. This was a peaceful meeting. The leaders wanted to establish a boundary line between the Dutch area and the

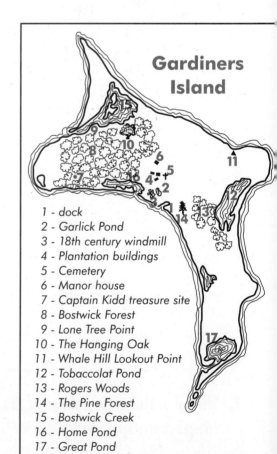

Gardiners Island

1 - dock
2 - Garlick Pond
3 - 18th century windmill
4 - Plantation buildings
5 - Cemetery
6 - Manor house
7 - Captain Kidd treasure site
8 - Bostwick Forest
9 - Lone Tree Point
10 - The Hanging Oak
11 - Whale Hill Lookout Point
12 - Tobaccolat Pond
13 - Rogers Woods
14 - The Pine Forest
15 - Bostwick Creek
16 - Home Pond
17 - Great Pond

English area of the island. This early boundary line divided Long Island.

This original boundary is close to the current one between Nassau and Suffolk. There is a historic marker to remind you of the early colonial boundaries.

In 1650, what we now call Nassau County (western Long Island) was the Dutch area. What we now know as Suffolk County (eastern Long Island) was the English territory. Which side of the boundary line do you live on?

Because of Cabot's early exploration, the English kings in the early 1600s believed that Long Island belonged to England. In 1639, an Englishman named Lion Gardiner bought an island off the eastern tip of Long Island from the Algonquians. Later, the island was given to him by charter from the king. A *charter* is a legal paper granting ownership.

Today this island still has the Gardiner name. Some people say that a famous pirate named Captain Kidd buried treasure there. Study the map on page 48.

Many of the early English settlers came from Connecticut. They moved their things in boats across Long Island Sound. In 1640, a Connecticut minister named John Youngs founded Southold. It is on the North Shore. Locate it on the map. Youngs and his people came for religious freedom.

In the same year, Southampton was settled by English people from Massachusetts. They were looking for good farming land.

Other early English settlements were Setauket, East Hampton, Huntington, and Smithtown. Find these places on the map.

Early wealthy settlers

Why do you think Long Island offered a better life than other places?

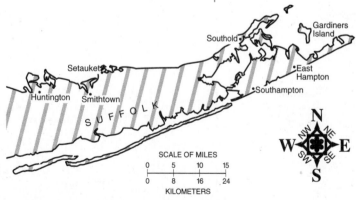

EASTERN LONG ISLAND

New Amsterdam Becomes New York

English towns quickly sprang up from Montauk Point to Gravesend. By 1664, English settlers outnumbered the Dutch colonists. England was now unhappy with the Nassau-Suffolk boundary line. *King Charles II* of England said that he owned all of Long Island.

Peter Stuyvesant surrenders New Amsterdam to the English.

Why are the people lining the way?

In 1662, the king sent a charter to Connecticut. The charter said Connecticut could take control of Long Island. The settlers were told to stop paying taxes to the Dutch.

In 1664, Charles II gave his brother, the Duke of York, the Dutch region of New Netherland. New Netherland included the colonies in Long Island, much of present-day New York State, and parts of New Jersey, Delaware, and Connecticut.

The Duke of York sent English ships to capture the Dutch fort at New Amsterdam. *Colonel Richard Nicolls*, the commanding officer, ordered Peter Stuyvesant to surrender to English rule. The other colonies in New Netherland were also taken over. The English renamed the region New York in honor of the Duke of York.

Life for the Colonists

Life on Long Island was hard for the colonists. People had to grow their own food, make their own clothes, and build their own houses.

The English houses were different from the Dutch homes. English settlers built their houses facing the sun. There were two stories with no stoop or porch. These homes were called *saltbox houses*. This was because they looked like the boxes salt was stored in.

A saltbox house

What clues do you have that this is a saltbox house?

Some old diaries tell us about the colonists' daily lives. Ebenezer Miller worked on a Long Island farm called Miller Place. He described his daily work in a diary.

In the early spring, he would plow or clear his fields. He would plant seeds of grain and corn. He mended fences and "went oystering."

Molly Cooper's diary tells what it was like to be a woman on Long Island in the 1700s. Molly lived in Cove Neck, which is on Oyster Bay. She baked bread and preserved food for winter. In the fall, she dried cherries and apples, dipped candles, and made soap.

She also cared for the bees and collected their honey. Molly wrote, "I am forced to climb a cherry tree and fetch the bees in my apron."

A Colonial woman makes soap.

What other chores would this woman have tended to in a typical day?

Like the Dutch, the English made many contributions to the life of Long Island. We owe our language to the English. Many everyday customs and habits were passed on from the English. How have the English influenced your community?

51

Recalling What You Read

Read the following statements. Some of them are more true about the English. Others are more true about the Dutch. You decide. On the line to the left, write **E** for English or **D** for Dutch.

_____ **1.** Settled the eastern part of Long Island.

_____ **2.** Came to Long Island to own land their children could inherit.

_____ **3.** Set up trading posts on the island of Manhattan.

_____ **4.** Heavily taxed their settlers.

_____ **5.** Were more successful at getting people to come to Long Island.

Think About It

1. If you were a Dutch person living on Long Island in 1664, tell how you would have felt when the English took over Long Island. Why would you feel this way?

_____

_____

_____

_____

2. How would Molly Cooper find her life on Long Island different today? How would it be the same? Why?

_____

_____

_____

_____

Problem Solver

In 1670, Daniel Denton wrote a brochure in London called *A Brief Description of New York, Formerly Called New Netherlands*. A major part of the brochure was written about Long Island. He wrote:

"The island is most of it a very good soyle...which they sowe and have very good increase of...Hemp, Flax, Pumpkins, Melons...The fruits natural to the Island are Mulberries...Grapes, great and small, Huckelberries, Cramberries, Plums of several sorts, Rosberries and Strawberries, of which last in such an abundance in June, that the fields and woods are died red...The greater part of the Island is very full of Timber, as Oaks, white and red, Walnut trees, Chestnut trees...."

1. What does he think of Long Island? _____

_____

_____

_____

2. Why do you think he wrote about Long Island this way? _____

_____

_____

_____

3. Write your own description of Long Island, based on what you've read so far.

_____

_____

_____

_____

Map Builder

Latitude and Longitude

To show the exact location of places on the Earth, imaginary lines called *latitude* and *longitude* are used. These lines are drawn in two directions.

The *Equator* is a line that runs east and west around the globe in the center between the North and South Poles. Lines that run parallel to it (in the same direction) are called lines of latitude. They tell how far a place is north or south of the Equator.

Lines that run north and south between the two poles are called meridians or lines of longitude. One of these lines is called the prime meridian and all other places are measured east and west of the prime meridian.

We measure the distance of these lines in degrees.

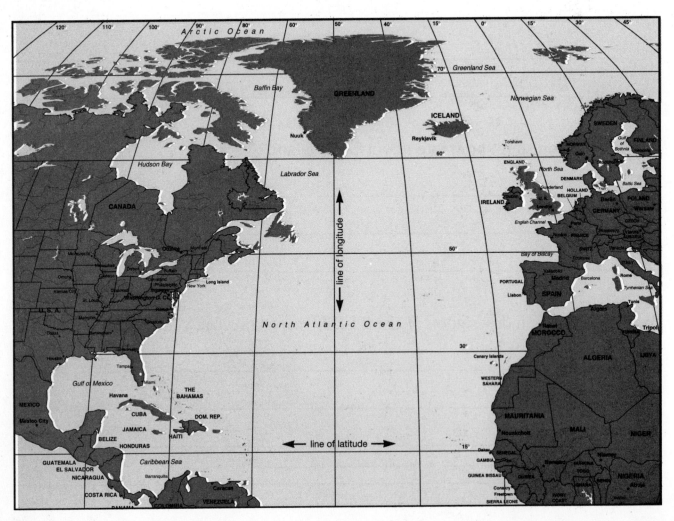

Look at the map on page 54 and see between which lines of latitude and longitude Long Island is located.

1. Now look at the lines of latitude and longitude nearest to England and Holland. Write a few sentences telling why you think that the explorers from these countries landed on or near Long Island.

_____

_____

_____

_____

_____

_____

_____

2. Is the weather on Long Island warmer or colder than that in England and Holland? Why?

_____

_____

_____

_____

_____

_____

Identify It

Below is a list of activities. Some of these things were done by the
Native Americans. Some were done by the colonists. Some were done
by both. Put an **N** next to those activities done by the Native Americans.
Place a **C** next to those done by the colonists. Put a **B** if done by both.

_____   kept vegetable gardens

_____   built wigwams

_____   made candles

_____   used sign language

_____   had children help out parents

_____   built dugout canoes

_____   hunted and fished

_____   shaved most of their hair

LI Inquiry

1. Describe how Algonquian, English, and Dutch life is similar to and
different from your life today.

_____

_____

_____

_____

2. Explain why you do or do not think that England had the right to claim New Netherland, including Long Island.

_____

_____

_____

_____

_____

Exploring Long Island

Trace Your Town's Name

The names of many Long Island communities are either from the Dutch, the Algonquians, or the English. What is the history behind your community's name? Write a short report on how your community got its name.

Study the names of places near where you live. Try to find five roads or places that were named by the Native Americans, Dutch, or English. Find out what these names mean. Add this information to your report.

Here are some other activities you might try:

1. Make a model of a Long Island Algonquian village.

2. Re-create an early Dutch or English village.

3. Read about the Shinnecock Village.

4. Visit the town of Hempstead (founded in 1644).

5. Tour a restored Long Island colonial home such as Rock Hall or Home Sweet Home.

Signing the Declaration of Independence

CHAPTER 7

The Road to Revolution

Before You Read

When England took over Long Island, the people thought life would get better. Why did they think things would be better under English rule? What kinds of things could go wrong?

NEW TERMS

- the Duke's Laws
- Stamp Act
- Boston Tea Party
- redcoats
- Second Continental Congress
- William Floyd
- Francis Lewis
- Philip Livingston
- Declaration of Independence
- Patriots
- Loyalists

Richard Nicolls was the new governor of New York. In 1665, he called a general meeting in Hempstead. Each of the Long Island towns was asked to send a representative. Representatives spoke for the people of each town.

The Duke's Laws

The purpose of this meeting was to set up a new government for Long Island. This government would be based on English law. These new rules were known as *the Duke's Laws*.

The colonists did not like the Duke's Laws. They had no voice in the writing of these new rules. The colonists were not given a chance to propose changes. They were told

The Duke's Laws are announced.

Are laws introduced this way today? Why not?

that this was the way things would be. They could no longer make up the laws for their own colony.

New trading laws were passed. These laws said that the colonies could not directly trade with any country except England. The English taxes were very high. The colonists could not afford this extra expense.

Things got even worse. The colonists were told that New York Harbor was the official port. Goods could enter or leave the colony only from this port.

Long Island had its own harbors. Bringing goods to New York Harbor was a long, unnecessary trip. It also meant that shipping cost more money.

The Road to the American Revolution

The unfair trading laws caused colonists to smuggle goods. Late at night, ships secretly left harbors like Oyster Bay and Glen Cove. This way, they could avoid the charges at New York Harbor. Smuggling on Long Island was very common. It caused the British to lose a great deal of money.

New York was just one of England's thirteen colonies. The other colonies were also upset about unfair English laws.

In 1765, England passed the *Stamp Act*. This meant that all of the colonists' legal papers had to have British stamps. This was expensive. The colonists complained that they were taxed but not represented in the English government. Finally, England did away with the stamp tax.

Colonists protest the Stamp Act.

What do you think they are burning?

The stamp tax was replaced by a heavy tax on tea. The colonists liked tea very much. They could not grow it in America. The new tea tax made them angry.

Colonists dressed as Native Americans dump tea overboard in Boston Harbor.

Why do you think this was called the "Boston Tea Party"?

One group fought back in 1773 by dumping the tea overboard in Boston Harbor. This was known as the *"Boston Tea Party."* The Long Island colonists did not participate in this "party." But many were sympathetic to those who did.

The famous tea party made the King of England, George III, furious. He sent thousands of British troops to America. These soldiers were nicknamed the *redcoats*. This was because of their bright red jackets. The arrival of the redcoats made the colonists even angrier.

Francis Lewis   Philip Livingston   William Floyd

How do you think these men were chosen to represent the people of Long Island?

Finally, the colonists decided to break away from England. In 1776, more than 50 colonists attended a special meeting in Philadelphia. This was called the *Second Continental Congress*.

Three of the men who represented New York were from Long Island. They were *William Floyd*, *Francis Lewis*, and *Philip Livingston*. Floyd was from Suffolk County. Livingston was from Kings County, or Brooklyn. Lewis lived in Queens.

These men, along with 53 others, signed the *Declaration of Independence* in 1776. This important document announced America's intent to be free of England.

The Loyalists and the Patriots

How did Long Islanders feel about all this? Many English colonists who lived on Eastern Long Island wanted freedom. They were called *Patriots*. Some of the colonists

Signing the Declaration of Independence

How did this document change life for Long Islanders? Did everyone benefit?

did not want to break away from England. They were called *Loyalists*.

The Loyalists felt it was to their advantage to remain under British rule. England was a strong military power. Being a British colony meant Americans would be taken care of. Great Britain protected her colonies.

There were also those who didn't care who made the rules. These people took a neutral position. They wanted peace — at any price.

But peace was not in store for Long Island!

Recalling What You Read

Look over the five events listed below. Which ones would the Patriots support? Which ones would the Loyalists support? On the lines to the left, put **P** for Patriots or **L** for Loyalists.

_____ **1.** Boston Tea Party

_____ **2.** Declaration of Independence

_____ **3.** Duke's Laws

_____ **4.** Stamp Act

_____ **5.** Second Continental Congress

Think About It

1. Do you think that the Duke's Laws were fair? Why or why not? Be specific with examples.

_____

_____

_____

_____

2. Imagine you are an English colonist on Long Island in the 1770s. Write a letter to a friend in England telling why you do or do not want to break away from England.

_____

_____

_____

_____

Problem Solver

The Declaration of Independence talked about freedom from England. Many people in the colonies were talking about a different kind of freedom. Jupiter Hammon was a slave living on Long Island. He was a part of the Lloyd family of Lloyd Manor, now Lloyd Neck. He was the first published African-American poet in America. Hammon wrote "An Address to the Negroes in the State of New York." In it he states: "I Acknowledge that liberty is a great thing, and worth seeking for."

1. What kind of liberty do you think Jupiter Hammon is talking about? How do you know?

_____

_____

_____

_____

_____

_____

_____

_____

_____

_____

Map Builder

Using a Polar Projection Map

A polar projection map shows you how the Earth looks if you were looking at it from above one of the poles. The map on this page is a North Polar map. The North Pole is the center of the map. North is the direction toward the center.

The straight lines are the *meridians* or *longitude* lines and the circular lines are the *parallels* or *latitude* lines. Polar maps help to determine distance and direction. Pilots use a polar map to help them fly the shortest distance in the least amount of time. One problem with the polar map is that the land farthest away from the center appears much larger than it really is. Also, its shape is not correct.

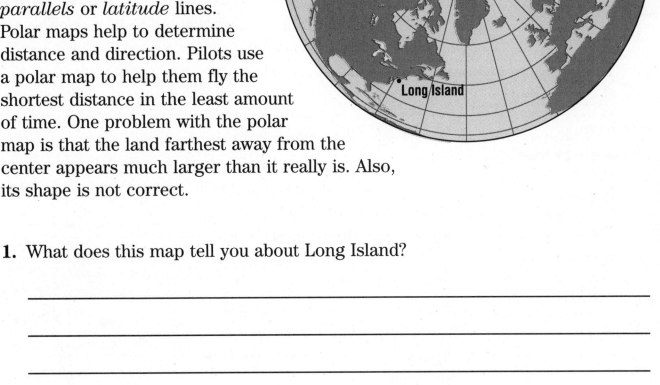
Long Island

1. What does this map tell you about Long Island?

_____

_____

_____

_____

_____

CHAPTER 8 Battles on Long Island

CHAPTER 8 Battles on Long Island

Before You Read

This chapter will describe Long Island's role at the beginning of the American Revolution. Look at the map on this page. Why do you think that the British would want to control Long Island?

NEW TERMS

- American Revolution
- Brooklyn Heights
- retreat
- Battle of Long Island
- General Nathaniel Woodhull
- whaleboat raid
- occupied

*L*ike the rest of the American colonies, Long Island was faced with war. Many colonists wanted their freedom from British rule. England did not want them to be free. The war that followed was called the *American Revolution*. Long Island played an important part in this war.

The Battle of Long Island

The British were eager to capture New York because it had a fine harbor. It also had a very important location. New York separated the New England colonies from the southern ones. (Check the map to the right.)

One of the first battles of the war was fought on Long Island. The battleground was *Brooklyn Heights*. This area overlooks New York Harbor.

The British sent a large army with 300 warships across the Atlantic. They set up camp on Staten Island to get organized after their long sea journey. Staten Island is south of Manhattan, in New York Bay.

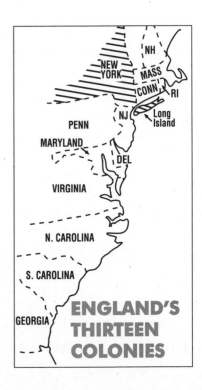

ENGLAND'S THIRTEEN COLONIES

The Battle of Long Island

Are you able to tell who the British are? Who the colonists are? How?

The leaders of the American army knew the British soldiers would soon be arriving. They tried to fortify Brooklyn Heights. They hoped to protect New York City.

The British, led by General William Howe, attacked on August 27, 1776. Twenty thousand British soldiers crossed New York Bay in flatboats.

The Patriots, led by General George Washington, fought bravely. But they were defeated. One group of American soldiers stood out for their bravery. These were the troops from Maryland.

They refused to *retreat* or back down. They kept fighting even though many of their men were killed. Their bravery allowed other Americans to escape.

Washington Leaves

Washington knew he had to get his men off Long Island. He planned to ferry them across the East River. The winds

General William Howe

How can you tell he is British and not a colonist?

General George Washington

Why was the Battle of Long Island a partial victory for him?

prevented British ships from sailing into the river. This kept the escape route open.

At night, in boats, Washington quietly moved his troops off Brooklyn Heights. A thick fog kept the British from discovering this. Most of Washington's troops reached Manhattan safely. They were then able to cross the Hudson and march into New Jersey.

If Washington's men had not escaped, the British might have won the war. The *Battle of Long Island* was a defeat for the colonists. It was also a victory. Do you understand why?

The Bravery of Nathaniel Woodhull

Before the battle, Washington told General Nathaniel Woodhull to travel to Queens. There, Woodhull guarded sheep and cattle. These animals were needed to feed the American army.

General Woodhull did not know about the defeat. British soldiers surrounded him. One officer ordered Woodhull to say "God save the king!" Instead, Woodhull

Retreat from Long Island

How can you tell that the artist wants you to know that it was a brave act?

70

said, "God save us all!" Furious, the officer slashed Woodhull with his sword. Woodhull died from an infection caused by that wound.

British Prisons and Whaleboat Raids

The British took control of Long Island. Their troops occupied forts in towns like Oyster Bay. They sent American soldiers and troublemakers to prison ships.

The British prison ships were terrible places. A thousand prisoners were crowded into each small ship. They were not given enough food, water, or air. The ships were filthy and people quickly became sick. To be put on one of these ships was almost a sure death sentence.

Many Long Islanders escaped to Connecticut. There, they organized whaleboat raids. A *whaleboat raid* was when a group of whaleboats would attack British forts on Long Island. Whaleboats were light and easy to handle. They were easy to hide until it was time for a raid.

Passage of the troops to Long Island

Was this the most efficient way to move the troops? How would it be done today?

At night, the whaleboats would cross Long Island Sound. American troops would burn and destroy British supplies. This would keep the supplies from reaching New York.

The Occupation of Long Island

The raiders would also take important Loyalist leaders as hostages. They would later exchange these hostages for imprisoned Americans.

Long Island was *occupied* by the British until the end of the American Revolution in 1783. The people of Long Island fought for independence in their own way. They helped win the war for American independence.

Recalling What You Read

Draw a line from the name to the words that describe it.

1. Staten Island

    a. leader of British Army

2. General George Washington

    b. camp of British Army

3. General William Howe

    c. British and American battleground

4. Brooklyn Heights

    d. leader of American Army

Think About It

1. Explain the important role that Long Island played in the American Revolution.

_____

_____

_____

_____

_____

2. The Battle of Long Island was both a victory and a defeat for the colonists. Explain this statement.

_____

_____

_____

_____

_____

Problem Solver

During the occupation, Long Island was forced to supply the British with food and shelter until the end of the war. Cattle, grain, and wood were very important to the British. The British soldiers were commanded to "take into your custody all the grain, forage, and creatures you can find on Long Island, being the property of persons actually in rebellion."

1. Why would cattle, grain, and wood be important to the British?

_____

_____

_____

_____

_____

2. Knowing these items were important, how could the Patriots hurt the British?

_____

_____

_____

_____

Map Builder

Reading a Historical Map

Sometimes, one picture is better than many words. Suppose you want to trace an explorer's route. What if you are trying to re-create a famous battle? A historical map could give you a good picture of both events.

Study the historical map on this page. It shows important information about the Battle of Long Island.

The map key or *legend* tells you what kind of information is on the map. Look at the legend on the map of the Battle of Long Island. Make sure you understand what the symbols mean.

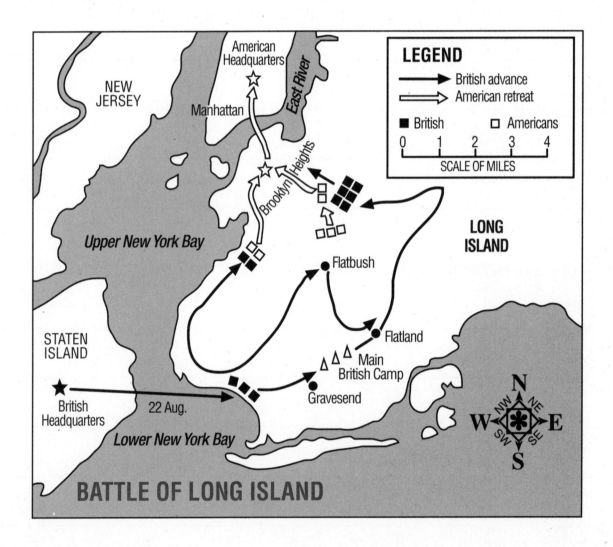

Using the map on page 74, complete the following questions.

1. The symbol ☐ stands for the _____ .

2. The British went in a(n) _____ direction
   from Staten Island toward Gravesend.

3. The British Headquarters were on Staten Island. The British then
   landed on Long Island. To do this they crossed over the _____ .

4. The _____ retreated through Brooklyn Heights.

5. Study the map. What conclusion or final statement can you make about the
   Battle of Long Island?

   _____

   _____

   _____

   _____

   _____

   _____

CHAPTER 9 Heroes and Spies

Before You Read

This chapter will tell you about the important role that spying played in Long Island history. Do you think that spying is a good or bad thing to do? Why?

NEW TERMS

- Nathan Hale
- Abraham Woodhull
- Austin Roe
- Caleb Brewster
- Anna "Nancy" Smith Strong
- Robert Townsend
- the Culper Spy Ring

*W*hile the British occupied Long Island, many New Yorkers worked as spies. Discovering secret information about an enemy is called *spying*. Spies played an important role in Long Island history.

The Actions of Nathan Hale

Spying was very dangerous work. If caught, a spy was killed immediately. Many spies were never caught, but others were.

One unlucky spy was *Nathan Hale*. Hale, a general in Washington's army, became a spy. General Washington needed to know what the British were doing in New York City.

Nathan Hale gave his life for his country.

Why was spying a courageous act?

76

Disguised as a Dutch schoolteacher, Nathan Hale went into British-occupied New York City. He was able to gather secret information. Just as Hale was about to return to Washington's camp, the British caught him.

The British decided to hang Nathan Hale. Some believe that Nathan Hale's last words were, "I only regret that I have but one life to lose for my country."

Nancy Strong's Laundry Line

Another spy was *Abraham Woodhull*, a farmer from Setauket. Woodhull was also assigned to spy in New York City. There, he watched British troop movements. He kept track of incoming and outgoing ships. He listened in taverns for news.

Woodhull then gave this information to a man named *Austin Roe*. Roe was a tavern owner in Setauket. He traveled weekly from Setauket to New York City pretending to shop for his tavern. His real mission was to meet secretly with Abraham Woodhull. This trip was very dangerous. The main roads were guarded by British troops.

Once back in Setauket, Roe passed the information he had gotten from Woodhull to *Caleb Brewster*. Brewster was a well-known whaleboat raider from Connecticut. Since British soldiers would recognize him, he had to be extra careful.

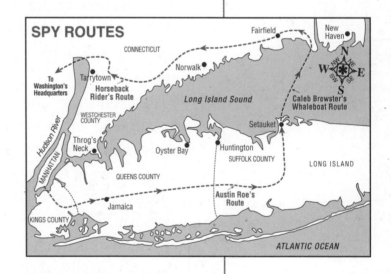

Brewster had to sail his whaleboat secretly into one of the coves north of Setauket. How did Brewster know which cove he should land in? He would study *Anna "Nancy" Smith Strong*'s laundry line.

On the line, Strong hung a black petticoat. Next to it she put some white handkrchiefs. The number of handkerchiefs was part of a secret code. This number told Brewster which cove he should land in.

Once Brewster received the information from Roe, he returned to Connecticut. There, a horseback rider would carry the information to General Washington.

The Culper Spy Ring

Spying was dangerous work. Spies were afraid that they would be killed if they were caught. For this reason, spies used secret code names. Woodhull's code name was Samuel Culper.

Another spy named *Robert Townsend* was called Culper, Jr. He and Woodhull were important members of what was known as *the Culper Spy Ring*. This spy ring included men and women whose identities we still don't know today.

In New York City, Townsend worked for a British newspaper. This gave him a good chance to move freely around the city. He could uncover secret information.

Townsend's family lived in a home in Oyster Bay called Raynham Hall. During the war, this house was occupied by British troops. Important English officers came to Raynham Hall.

Townsend was able to discover some of their secrets. You can visit the scene of this early spy drama. Raynham Hall is open to the public.

Spying went on during the seven years that the British occupied New York City. Elsewhere in the colonies, the American troops were winning battle after battle. A major victory for the Americans was when the British surrendered at Yorktown, Virginia, in 1781.

Finally, in 1783, British and American leaders signed the Treaty of Paris. This ended the revolution. The Americans had won. The colonies were finally free of British rule. The Culper Spy Ring helped the Americans defeat the British.

Recalling What You Read

How good are you at finding important information? First, complete the sentences below. Then study the "Word Search" on page 80. The answers you wrote on the lines in questions 1 to 7 will appear there.

1. As a reporter, this spy was free to look for secret information in New York City. His name was

   _____.

2. This spy and many others were part of the _____ Spy Ring.

3. A successful whaleboat raider turned spy was _____.

4. This spy regretted that he had but one life to lose for his country. His name was

   _____.

5. A farmer from Setauket who spied on the British in New York City was

   _____.

6. This tavern owner turned spy made regular trips to New York City. His name was

   _____.

7. An important document that ended the American Revolution was the

   _____.

Word Search

You can find the answers to "Recalling What You Read" in this puzzle. The words you're looking for may be printed across, up, down, backwards, or diagonally. Circle the words.

A	M	A	O	J	R	T	L	A	L	M	G	D	A	E	T
L	L	U	H	D	O	O	W	M	A	H	A	R	B	A	R
C	T	U	U	A	B	D	R	O	B	T	L	N	C	R	E
A	X	A	G	H	E	T	O	S	L	V	W	J	A	M	A
L	O	L	S	G	R	L	T	O	R	E	P	L	U	C	T
E	O	B	P	H	T	P	A	B	R	E	W	T	I	L	Y
B	T	I	Y	T	T	X	F	H	A	L	T	Y	R	I	O
B	S	B	D	E	O	G	O	B	N	N	H	O	F	S	F
R	H	L	T	R	W	F	D	A	T	A	I	L	O	L	P
E	O	E	O	R	N	I	T	S	U	A	H	K	R	A	A
W	T	D	F	I	S	G	E	O	R	G	E	T	T	N	R
S	C	T	A	N	E	C	I	R	E	M	A	O	A	D	I
T	U	C	R	L	N	L	O	N	G	T	O	W	F	N	S
E	L	P	E	R	D	T	E	A	M	O	N	N	M	I	T
R	E	L	P	E	R	D	L	T	A	R	T	E	A	D	Z

Think About It

1. Spies played a very important role during the Revolutionary War. Explain why this statement is true or false.

   _____

   _____

   _____

   _____

   _____

2. If you had lived during the Revolutionary Period, which spy you would have liked to have been? Why? Choose from Nathan Hale, Abraham Woodhull, Austin Roe, Caleb Brewster, Nancy Strong, or Robert Townsend.

   _____

   _____

   _____

   _____

   _____

Problem Solver

Women were part of the Culper Spy Ring. Abraham Woodhull wrote a letter to George Washington about one such spy, Agent 355. He wrote "I intend to visit 727 (New York) before long and I think by the assistance of 355...I shall be able to outwit them all."

Although not proven, it is said Agent 355 was coded as "Lady." She was able to tell Townsend that the British knew of the French arrival at Newport, Rhode Island. She also told him that the British fleet would go to Throg's Neck and set sail for Newport, Rhode Island.

1. Why do you think Abraham Woodhull had such faith in Agent 355? Make a list of the qualities you think a successful spy should have.

_____

_____

_____

_____

_____

2. In what ways was spying patriotic? When is spying not patriotic?

_____

_____

_____

_____

_____

Map Builder

Globe

A globe is a model of the Earth. It shows the land and water areas on the Earth. It is round and shows the shape of the Earth. Globes are made so you can turn them, just like the Earth turns.

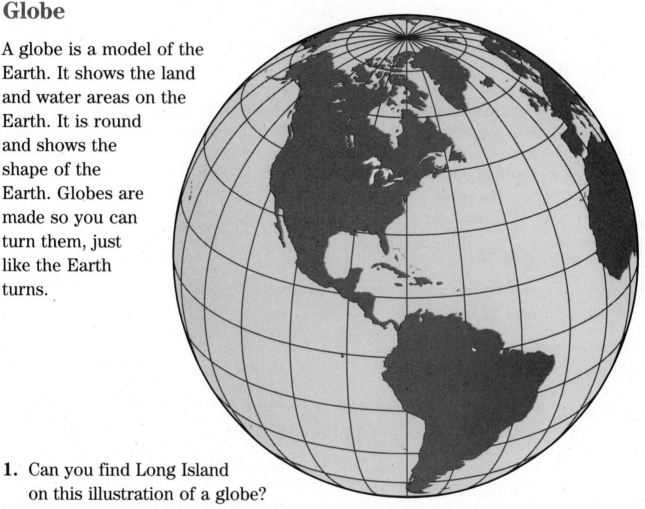

1. Can you find Long Island on this illustration of a globe?

_____

_____

2. Describe its location in relation to the rest of the United States and Europe.

_____

_____

_____

_____

Who Am I?

Study the names below. Each one has an identifying letter.
Match the letters to the numbered statements below.

a–**Robert Townsend**   b–**Caleb Brewster**
c–**Richard Nicolls**   d–**William Floyd**   e–**Nathan Hale**

_____ 1. "I was governor of New York. I called the meeting that explained the Duke's Laws."

_____ 2. "I represented Long Island when I signed the Declaration of Independence."

_____ 3. "I was a whaleboat raider. I was also a spy during the Revolutionary War."

_____ 4. "I was hanged by the British as a spy. I only regret that I have but one life to lose for my country."

_____ 5. "I was a spy for George Washington. My home, Raynham Hall, can be visited today."

LI Inquiry

1. Long Island played a key role in the colonists' victory in the American Revolution. Support this statement with at least three specific examples.

_____

_____

_____

_____

_____

2. Pretend you were either a Patriot or Loyalist during the Revolutionary War. Write in your diary, telling why the war is being fought and about a recent event on Long Island.

_____

_____

_____

_____

_____

_____

Exploring Long Island

Discover Your Town's Role in the Revolution

Long Island played an important role in the Revolutionary War. A book called *Long Island in the American Revolution* further explains that role. Use this book or another like it as a starting point.

In your notebook, describe the part your town played in the Revolutionary War. If there's too much information, pick a few key events. If your area isn't mentioned, choose a town nearby.

You might also work together with some other students. Create a short play about one or several of the events. Act it out for the rest of the class.

Growth and Developmen

Grumman workers assemble airplane parts.

CHAPTER 10

Whaling and Fishing

Before You Read

This chapter tells about the different ways in which fishing helped many Long Islanders to grow richer. Why would fishing be an important occupation on Long Island?

NEW TERMS

- scrimshaw
- baleen
- onshore whaling
- offshore whaling
- harpoon
- Marine Mammal Protection Act

*T*he Revolutionary War was over. People on Long Island could lead normal lives again. They eagerly returned to fishing and farming.

Fishing was an important part of the Native American way of life. The Algonquians taught the early settlers how to catch fish and shellfish. Later, the settlers improved on the Algonquians' methods.

The Importance of Whaling

In the 1800s, whaling was a good way to earn a living on Long Island. Many valuable products were made from whales. From the whale *blubber* or fat came oil. This oil was burned in lamps and used to grease machinery. Spermaceti was taken from the head of the whale. This wax was used to make candles. Ambergris came from the whale's intestines. It was an ingredient in expensive perfume.

Even the whale's teeth were used. Sailors passed the time during long voyages by carving designs or pictures into polished whale teeth. They filled the

Oil-burning lamp

What other products were derived from whales?

engraved lines with colored ink. These carvings, called *scrimshaw*, are very valuable today.

The whale's bones were also used. Whalebone is called *baleen*. Baleen was very useful. Buttons and stays on women's corsets were made from it.

Besides these products, whaling helped other Long Island businesses. Barrels were needed to hold whale oil. Blacksmiths forged whaling tools. Ship building increased. Farmers supplied and sold food to whaling ships.

Different Ways to Go Whaling

There were two ways to hunt whales. One way was called *onshore whaling*. The other way was *offshore whaling*.

Here's how the onshore method worked. A whale watch would be set up by the people of a town. Whales sometimes swam near the shore. People took turns looking for them.

The whale watcher sat on top of a large sand dune. If a whale was spotted, an alarm was sounded. The whalers rushed to the beach and their whaleboats.

Offshore whaling took place in the ocean. A boat steerer kept watch on the whale and its movements. The steerer directed the whaleboat toward the animal.

Scrimshaw

How do you know this is scrimshaw?

Barrels are used to hold oil.

What kind of oil are these barrels holding?

*Men harpoon
a whale.*

**Why are all the
people in the boat
needed to kill the
whale?**

When the whale surfaced, the harpooner tried to
throw a harpoon into it. A *harpoon* is a giant spear with
ropes attached. Once the harpoon was in the whale, the
whalers pulled their boats closer. They could then lance
and kill the animal.

Whales put up a good fight. Often, they pulled boats for
miles before tiring. Their great tails could smash a boat or
turn it over. Once killed, the whale was towed back to
shore. Its blubber was cut off and boiled for oil.

Offshore whaling became very profitable for ship
owners. The ship owners sent ships all over the world in
search of whales. It sometimes took two or three years for
a whaling ship to return. The captain waited until he had a
full cargo of whale oil and other products.

The Decline of Whaling

Sag Harbor and Cold Spring Harbor were Long Island's
busiest whaling ports. One year, Sag Harbor sent out more
than 80 whaling ships.

In 1859, the discovery of petroleum oil in Pennsylvania hurt the whaling industry. Petroleum oil was easier and cheaper to get than whale oil. It was also more useful.

The discovery of gold in California in 1849 also hurt the whaling industry. Many men in whaling ships traveled to California in search of gold. They did not return to whaling.

The number of whales was greatly reduced by hunting. In recent years, laws have been passed to protect whales. The *Marine Mammal Protection Act* forbids the sale of any whale products.

Fishing on Long Island

Since the earliest days, fishing has been important to Long Islanders. Like the Native Americans, the early settlers included fish in their meals.

Fishing became profitable when the settlers caught more than they needed for their own survival. They sold this extra catch in New York City. The fishers transported the fish in special boats that had saltwater tanks.

A lobster boat

Why would lobstering be a profitable business on Long Island?

What kinds of fish swim in Long Island waters? A large variety can be found. There are flounder, weakfish, porgies, bluefish, codfish, and bass. There are giant tunas that weigh several hundred pounds.

As you know, Long Island has many bays.

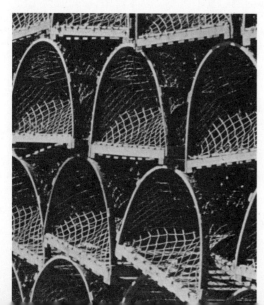

Lobster pots

Find out how lobsters are caught. How is it different from catching fish?

Shellfish such as oysters, clams, and scallops are found in these bays. Lobsters are also caught in the North Atlantic.

Oyster Bay was named after the oysters found there. Blue Point was famous for the high quality of its oysters. The Great South Bay supplies clams.

Raising scallops is another big shellfish business. Scallops collected from the bottom of Peconic Bay are well known for their good taste.

Long Island fishers still supply fish to New York City and their own island. Fresh fish are featured at many local restaurants. Sport fishing is a popular sideline of the fishing business.

In 1985, there were 8,372 commercial fishing boats in Long Island waters. Each year, about fifty million pounds of fish are caught. This catch sells for between fifty and sixty million dollars.

For centuries, fishing has provided food and employment for the people of Long Island.

Fishing boats at Montauk

Is Montauk a good place to go fishing? Why do you think so?

CHAPTER review 10

Recalling What You Read

Write **T** next to each statement that is true.
Write **F** next to each sentence that is false.

_____ **1.** Whaling was a very profitable business in the 1800s.

_____ **2.** The two ways to hunt whales are "harpoon" and "baleen" whaling.

_____ **3.** One reason whales were hunted was to obtain oil.

_____ **4.** One kind of fish not found in Long Island waters is the flounder.

Think About It

1. The whale was very important to the economy of Long Island in the 1800s. Support this statement in a paragraph.

_____

_____

_____

_____

_____

2. Explain the difference between onshore and offshore whaling.

_____

_____

_____

_____

_____

Problem Solver

Women also went "whaling" in the 1800s. At least 48 Long Island captains' wives shipped out on whalers, ocean-going coastal ships, and coastal trading ships. Martha Smith Brewer Brown was one of these women. She wrote letters to her daughter about her experiences. Two of her letters appear below:

October 28, 1847

"Two months now since we left home…Everyone is occupied while I am sitting by an open window nearly two square, sometimes sewing, sometimes knitting, then reading, then attempting to sing, now looking out upon the works of nature, no, of God, watching the birds as they skip…from wave to wave."

October 29, 1847

"Today, I have been making pumpkin pies…I have made four kinds of pies since we have been out…Oh for one sweet kiss from my dear Ella…Why did I leave her at home?…It is necessary to go for one voyage to know what we want. I think the next time I shall enjoy it much better…"

(from *She Went a Whaling*)
ed. by Anne MacKay
Oysterponds Historical Society, 1993

1. What is Martha Smith Brewer Brown doing with her time? Why do you think she went on the whaling ship?

_____

_____

_____

_____

_____

_____

Map Builder

The Sailor's Map

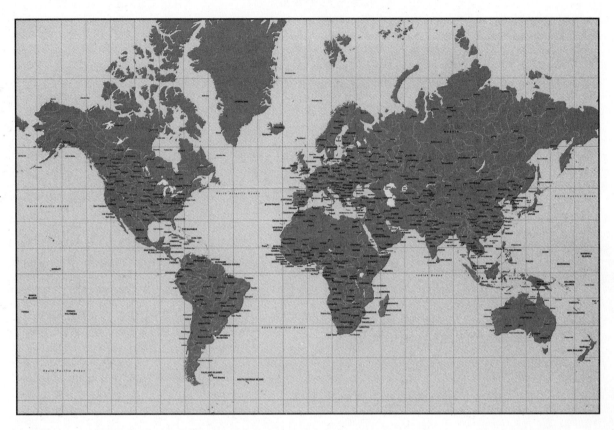

This map is called a Mercator Projection. It is a flat map of the Earth. Since the Earth is really round, not everything on the map is shown in the same shape and size as it is on a globe. On a globe the lines of longitude curve. They all meet at the North and South Poles. On this map they are shown as straight parallel lines. On a globe the lines of latitude on the top and bottom are shorter than those in the middle. On a Mercator Projection map, they are all the same length. The Mercator Projection correctly shows direction from one place to another.

1. Explain why you think the Mercator Projection is called the "sailor's map."

_____

_____

_____

_____

_____

CHAPTER 11

Farming–Past and Present

Before You Read

This chapter will explain how farming was and still remains important to Long Islanders. What crops do you see growing on Long Island today? Where do you see them? Why?

NEW TERMS

- Sheep Parting Day
- grist mill
- white Pekin duck
- harrow
- scythe

*F*arming is an important part of Long Island's history. The Native Americans grew many vegetables. The early settlers were farmers. In addition to vegetables, the settlers raised livestock. This included sheep, cattle, poultry, and other farm animals.

Raising Livestock

Raising livestock was popular and profitable. People in New York City needed meat. Cattle and sheep could be sent there by boat.

In the early years, Hempstead Plains, the central portion of what is now Nassau County, was used as a giant pasture.

A Long Island farm

Why did Long Island become an important farming community?

It was some 60,000 acres in size. In addition, marsh grass grew freely along the South Shore. The grass was used as feed and bedding for livestock.

Peninsulas made good cattle and sheep pens. Fences were built across the narrow neck of the peninsula. The livestock was then left to graze. Many farmers shared the cost of the fencing. They then had the right to share the pen.

Sheep Parting Day

How did the owners keep track of their livestock? Once a year, there was a holiday called *Sheep Parting Day*. At this time, all the livestock were herded into a fenced area. Owners then identified their animals by special ear marks.

These identifying marks were recorded in the town book. They were passed on from father to son. Sheep Parting Day was like a big festival. There was food, drink, games, and entertainment.

Different Crops on Long Island

After the Revolutionary War, New York City grew rapidly. There was a great demand for flour. Long Island farmers began to raise wheat, rye, and corn to make flour.

These grains were ground into flour at a *grist mill*. Inside the mills were huge grindstones. The mills were powered by water or the wind.

By the late 1800s, most of the nation's wheat was being grown in the Midwest. Long Island farmers turned their

A grist mill wheel in Great Neck

What is the purpose of the turning wheel?

grain fields into gardens. They grew fruits and vegetables that helped feed New York City's growing population. This is still true today.

Strawberries, asparagus, Brussels sprouts, cucumbers, and cauliflower grow well in eastern Long Island. Other island-grown fruits and vegetables are green beans, cabbage, spinach, corn, lettuce, grapes, tomatoes, and potatoes. About 8,000 acres of land are used just to grow potatoes.

Another well-known Long Island farm product is the duckling. Ducks are raised around Riverhead and Moriches Bay. This industry began in 1873. A sea captain brought seven *white Pekin ducklings* back to Long Island from China.

Today, about five percent of the nation's ducks are raised on Long Island. Chickens, turkeys, geese, and eggs are other local poultry products.

Some Long Island farmers have nurseries. Here they grow and sell flowers, shrubs, and trees. People buy plants and trees to make their homes and yards more pleasant.

White Pekin ducks

Do you think the Algonquins ate Pekin ducks? Why or why not?

Life on the Farm

Today, the farmer's job is made easier by modern equipment. Farming in the 1800s and early 1900s was a different story.

Life on the farm was not easy. Jobs were done according to the season. Plowing was the first big spring job. Farmers used horses or oxen to pull their plows.

The soil in a plowed field had many *clods* or lumps of dirt. A *harrow* was used to break up the clods. It made the soil smooth. Farmers then planted seeds.

In the summer, the hay was harvested. At first, hay was mowed with a *scythe*. This was a sharp, heavy tool that took careful handling. Later on, hay was mowed with a machine drawn by a horse. After mowing, the hay was left out in the sun to dry. It was then raked into big bundles and pitched into hay wagons.

Women helped in the fields, tended the animals, and preserved food. Since doctors were scarce, many women learned to use plants and herbs for medicine.

Today, Long Island has more people living in urban areas than on farms. Each year, many acres of rich farmland are developed into sites for new homes and businesses. Even so, farming is still important to Long Island's economy. Suffolk is the leading agricultural county in New York State.

A scythe

How do you think the scythe was used?

A painting of a Long Island homestead

Would you find this scene on Long Island today? Why or why not?

Recalling What You Read

Look through the chapter for answers to complete the following sentences. Write your answers in the blanks below.

1. Three types of livestock raised on Long Island were _____ ,

   _____ , and _____ .

2. Grain was ground into flour at a _____ .

3. Three crops grown by farmers on Long Island today are _____ ,

   _____ , and _____ .

4. People sell flowers and shrubs in _____ .

5. Two tools used by farmers in the 1800s were a _____

   and a _____ .

Think About It

1. Describe what an average day on a Long Island farm in the 1800s would have been like. Include the chores that needed to be done.

   _____

   _____

   _____

2. Today Long Island is still an important agricultural area of New York. Support this statement with specific examples of the agricultural products of today.

   _____

   _____

   _____

Problem Solver

Less than twenty years ago, people did not think that quality wine could be made on Long Island. Today, wine experts claim that the wine produced on Long Island is outstanding.

There are 14 wineries and about 50 vineyards on the East End forks of Long Island. They have planted 1,600 acres of grapes. Long Island produces three million bottles of wine each year.

1. Research and find out the reason that Long Island has been able to develop these wineries in the last twenty years.

_____

_____

_____

_____

_____

_____

_____

2. Explain the effect the wineries have had on Long Island. Have they been a valuable contribution to Long Island?

_____

_____

_____

_____

_____

_____

Map Builder

Census Map

A census map is based on information collected by the government. Look at the maps on the next page. They show changes in Long Island county boundaries from 1880 to the present day. Keep in mind that Kings and Queens counties are now part of New York City.

1. Write a short paragraph describing the changes in census boundaries over time. How would you explain these changes?

   _____

   _____

   _____

   _____

   _____

   _____

   _____

2. Focus on the current boundaries of Suffolk County. Some citizens on the east end want to form their own county, called Peconic. Why do you think the people here would want their own separate county?

   _____

   _____

   _____

   _____

   _____

   _____

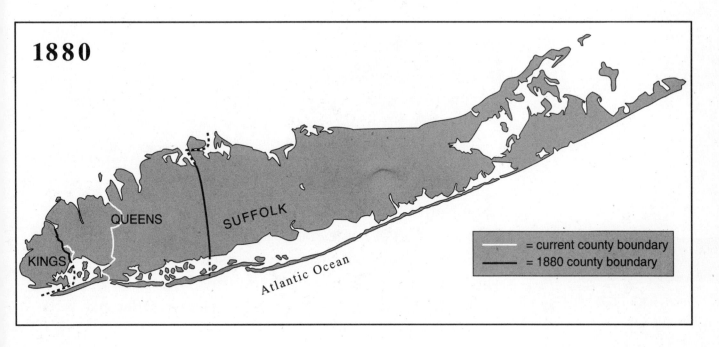

1880

QUEENS   SUFFOLK

KINGS

Atlantic Ocean

= current county boundary
= 1880 county boundary

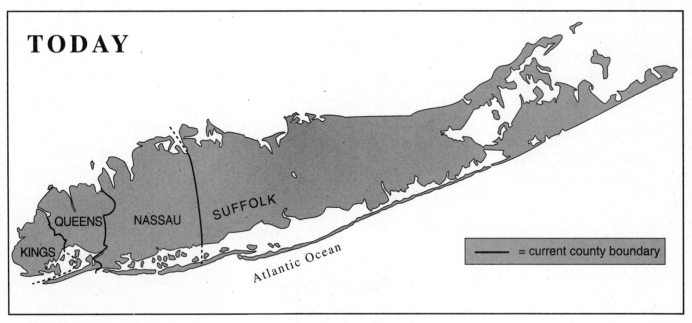

TODAY

QUEENS   NASSAU   SUFFOLK

KINGS

Atlantic Ocean

= current county boundary

3. Where would you place Long Island's new county? Draw a line to indicate the boundary between Suffolk and Peconic.

CHAPTER 12

Transportation – Old and New

Before You Read

Imagine what your life would be like without modern transportation. This means you wouldn't have cars, trains, or airplanes to ride. How would it change your life?

NEW TERMS

- King's Highway
- turnpike
- toll
- William K. Vanderbilt
- Robert Moses
- Brooklyn Bridge
- John A. Roebling
- Long Island Rail Road

*T*he Native Americans of Long Island were without cars or buses. To get somewhere, they usually walked or traveled in canoes. Their early paths were used by the Dutch and English settlers. Many roads you travel on today were originally trails used by Native Americans. Montauk Highway was one such trail.

Colonial Roads

In the 1700s, an important road was built on Long Island. It was called the *King's Highway* and ran through Brooklyn to Jamaica, Queens. Later, this road was extended to Sag Harbor in Suffolk. Long Island's modern system of highways basically follows the roads that existed in colonial days.

George Washington's Trip

Most people walked or traveled by horse in the 1700s. Wealthy people could afford carriages. In 1772, a stagecoach service carried passengers between Brooklyn Ferry and Sag

An early form of transportation

What types of problems do you think Long Island had with its roads in the 1700s?

Harbor. With overnight stops, this 120-mile trip took three days!

In 1790, President George Washington toured Long Island by stagecoach. He wanted to thank Long Islanders for their bravery during the American Revolution. You can follow his route on the map on this page. With overnight stops, this trip took the president five days!

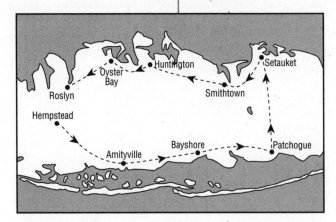

George Washington's visit

Why do you think he visited the places that he did?

The Building of Turnpikes

In the 1800s, some roads were built or improved by private companies. These new roads were called *turnpikes*. People were charged a fee, called a *toll*, to travel on them.

The first Long Island turnpike linked Jamaica, in Queens, with Rockaway. Construction began in 1806. More turnpikes were built connecting Jamaica with other parts of Long Island. Two of these were the Jericho Turnpike and the North Hempstead Turnpike.

Farmers, carrying their goods to market, used the early turnpikes. Peddlers also traveled these roads. They went from house to house with a cart or backpack full of things to sell.

In the late 1800s, horse-pulled vehicles were commonly used. These included the buggy, surrey, and sleigh. Heavy-duty wagons carried crops and supplies.

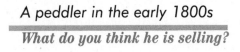

A peddler in the early 1800s

What do you think he is selling?

A family goes for a ride in the late 1800s.

Do you think they were going on a ride for pleasure? Why or why not?

The Building of Highways

The first concrete highway in the world was built on Long Island in 1908. Millionaire *William K. Vanderbilt* financed the 45-mile highway from Queens to Lake Ronkonkoma.

A toll of $2 prevented many people from using this highway. Some of those that did may have been driving a Model T Ford. This early automobile was produced by Henry Ford in 1908.

A public highway system was developed in the 1920s. *Robert Moses* created a state highway system that connected all parts of Long Island. He was responsible for planning such modern highways as the Northern and Southern State Parkways. These parkways made it easier for people to visit Long Island recreational areas. They also made it easier to drive to homes on the island.

Bridges Connect Long Island

Bridges joined Long Island with the rest of New York. The first of these, the *Brooklyn Bridge*, was completed in 1883. It connected Brooklyn and Manhattan. Farmers could then bring their products into the city without a long ferry delay.

The building of the Brooklyn Bridge amazed the world. It was the largest suspension bridge ever built up to that time. The engineers for the project were *John A.* and *Emily Roebling*, German immigrants.

Early on the job, Roebling had an accident and died. His son, Colonel Washington A. Roebling, finished the project. Chester A. Arthur, then President of the United States, attended the bridge's opening.

Other bridges were built, such as the Queensboro and Throg's Neck Bridges. Tunnels were also constructed to link Long Island to New York City. These were used by cars and trucks and later by subways. Building such tunnels as the Queens-Midtown Tunnel was difficult and dangerous work.

The Long Island Rail Road

The *Long Island Rail Road* did much to join the island with New York City. The railroad began in the early 1800s as a plan to link New York to Boston. At that time, it was difficult to reach Boston through Connecticut.

The plan was for passengers to take the train from Brooklyn to Greenport. A steamship would then bring them to Stonington, Connecticut. From there, another train would take them to Boston. This project was completed in 1844.

At first, a ride on the train was a real adventure. Trains went ten miles an

Early commuters ride the Long Island Rail Road.

Where might they be going? Why do you think that?

hour. That was considered fast. Locomotives were powered by steam. Sparks from the smokestack could ruin clothes and start fires.

Farmers didn't like the railroads passing through their property. Trains often killed stray livestock. In revenge, farmers would soap railroad tracks. They also burned train stations.

In 1848, a railroad route was built through Connecticut to Boston. The Long Island Rail Road lost most of its business. Many sidelines from the main track were built during this period.

About 30 independent railroads were started. Many of them had very short runs. There was too much competition for any of them to make money. They did create a lot of different routes. Many of these routes are still in use today.

Finally, by 1882, all of the independent railroads were combined. The Long Island Rail Road controlled everything.

Now, the Long Island Rail Road was doing a good business. It offered special freight services to farmers. It brought people on vacation to Long Island. Improved railroad service encouraged people to live on the island.

Today, the Long Island Rail Road is used mostly by commuters. These are people who live on Long Island and work in another part of the island or in New York City.

The Long Island Rail Road is one of the most active lines in the nation. It schedules more than 700 trains daily. Approximately 272,000 people are passengers on these trains.

Recalling What You Read
Finish each of the following sentences with information from the chapter.

1. The train system used by most people on Long Island is called the

_____ .

2. People had to pay a toll to use a road called a _____ .

3. The first turnpike built on Long Island was between _____

and _____ .

4. Built by the settlers in the 1700s, an important road on Long Island was called the

_____ .

5. The bridge completed in 1883 that connected Brooklyn and Manhattan was the

_____ .

Think About It

1. How is traveling on Long Island today different than in the 1700s?

_____

_____

_____

_____

2. Explain why some people didn't like the Long Island Rail Road.

_____

_____

_____

Problem Solver

You have been hired as an engineer to decide where to build a new highway on Long Island. First, you need to find out where the new highway is most needed. Find a road map of Long Island. Decide where to put the new road. Explain why you have chosen the new route.

_____

_____

_____

_____

_____

_____

_____

_____

_____

_____

Figuring Out a Road Map

Long Island has a modern system of highways and parkways. How can you find your way through this concrete maze? The best way is to look at a road map.

People use road maps to get from one place to another. Road maps can also help you find places of interest.

Like other types of maps, a road map uses symbols and has a key. Look at the key on the map below. Which symbol shows an airport? Which one stands for a state park?

Road maps use different lines to show the different types of roads. Thick lines are used for major roads. Thin lines indicate smaller roads. The road number may appear inside a symbol. This tells you if the road is an interstate or county road.

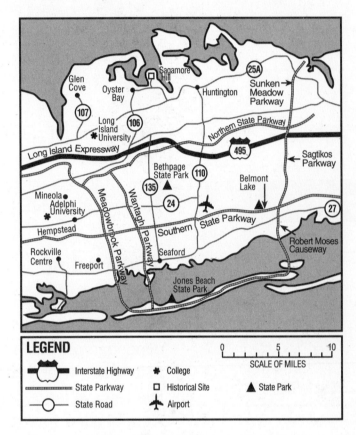

1. Explain why it is important for a road map to show the different types of roads as well as the route of the roads.

   _____

   _____

   _____

   _____

Before You Read

In this chapter you will see how transportation helped new industry to grow on Long Island. Can you think of how transportation could help new industry grow?

NEW TERMS

- Civil War
- Glenn Curtiss
- aviator
- Charles A. Lindbergh
- Grumman Corporation

*N*ew forms of transportation brought more people to Long Island. As Long Island grew in population, it also grew in new industry or business. Let's consider how transportation affected Long Island industry.

Shipbuilding

In the 18th and 19th centuries, there was a great need for boats and ships. Before modern roads, farmers depended on boats to carry products to New York City. Fishermen used boats to travel bays and oceans. Whalers had to have large, well-built ships. Ironclad battleships were needed for wars fought in and out of the United States.

To meet these needs, Long Island became an important shipbuilding center. Remember that the Long Island coastline has many protected harbors. This makes it a good place for shipyards.

In the 1800s, Cold Spring Harbor and Port Jefferson were important shipbuilding areas. The Brooklyn Navy Yard also became very well known.

The Brooklyn Navy Yard

One of the famous *Civil War* battleships, the *Monitor*, was built in 1862 in the Brooklyn Navy Yard. The Civil War

The Old Brooklyn Navy Yard

Why do you think this shipbuilding center is now closed?

(1861 to 1865) was fought between northern and southern states over slavery and other issues.

The Brooklyn Navy Yard also produced the battleship *Maine*. In 1898, the *Maine* blew up in Havana Harbor. You will learn more about the *Maine* when you study American history.

In the 1900s, Americans fought in two major world wars. These were World War I (1914 to 1918) and World War II (1939 to 1945).

Giant battleships were built for World War II in the Brooklyn Navy Yard. One of these was the *U.S.S. Missouri*. The *Independence* and *Saratoga* aircraft carriers were also produced there. The Brooklyn Navy Yard closed in 1968. Today many kinds of industries are located on its former site.

Currently, most of Long Island's boat building is limited to pleasure boats. Greenport is one of the small boat building areas servicing fishing and pleasure boats. This industry provides jobs to many Long Islanders.

There are other types of businesses and jobs related to

The U.S.S. Missouri

How does this ship differ from the ones in the Old Brooklyn Navy Yard?

ships. Shipping is one of them. Large cargo boats come to New York from ports all over the world. These boats must be unloaded. The products must be stored in warehouses. Then the products are delivered all over the United States. More products are received and shipped out from Brooklyn than any other port on the East Coast.

Aviation

Aviation is another area of transportation that has created new industry for Long Island. The island is a good place for airplanes and airfields because of its geography. There are long, flat areas that provide fine landing fields. Landing is made easier because Long Island is surrounded by water. Pilots don't have to worry about mountains or other obstacles.

There are two major airports and other minor airfields on Long Island. John F. Kennedy International and La Guardia Airports are located in Queens. They host many national and international flights each day. Kennedy is one of the world's busiest airports. Suffolk County's MacArthur Airport is the largest airport on eastern Long Island. Many island residents have jobs related to the airports.

Long Island's aviation history began in 1909 with *Glenn Curtiss*. This daring *aviator* flew his plane, the *Golden Flier,* an amazing 25 miles across the Hempstead Plains. This pioneer airplane looked like a big box kite.

Curtiss' flight took place only six years after Wilbur and Orville Wright's historic flight in Kitty Hawk, North Carolina. Wilbur traveled 852 feet in 59 seconds.

Curtiss found Long Island a good place for testing planes. He built an airplane factory in Garden City. His workers produced planes that were used to fight in World War I.

The most famous flight from Long Island was in May 1927. From Roosevelt Field in Garden City, *Charles A. Lindbergh* flew the *Spirit of St. Louis* across the Atlantic Ocean. This was the first nonstop flight from New York to Paris, France.

Lindbergh traveled 3,600 miles in 33 hours. The world cheered his heroic feat. Today, Roosevelt Field is the site of a popular shopping mall.

Charles A. Lindbergh

Why was his accomplishment important?

Wartime Construction

Fighter plane building was an important industry during World War II. As many as 15,000 military planes were built by the Republic Aviation Corporation near Farmingdale. This company later became Fairchild Republic.

During the war years, Republic had more than 20,000 employees. Many of these were women because the men were fighting. Republic's most famous Army fighter plane was called the Thunderbolt.

Another very important airplane factory during World War II was the *Grumman Company*. Its plants were located in Bethpage and Calverton.

During wartime, Grumman produced about 600 planes a month. Well-known Grumman planes were the Wildcat, and later, the Panther. The Wildcat was a World War II naval fighter plane. The Panther was used as a carrier jet plane.

Both the shipbuilding and aircraft industries continued to bring new jobs and opportunities to the people of Long Island for a long time.

The Wildcat

Do fighter planes still look like this? How are they different?

CHAPTER review 13

Recalling What You Read

Complete the sentences below with information from the chapter.

1. Two major airports on Long Island are _____

   and _____ .

2. One reason why boats were built on Long Island in the 18th and 19th centuries was

   _____ .

3. One community in Long Island that had a shipyard in the 1800s was

   _____ .

Think About It

1. The Grumman Corporation was very important to Long Island's economic growth. Explain why this was so.

   _____

   _____

   _____

   _____

2. Of the industries mentioned in this chapter, which do you think are the most important to Long Island's economy today? Why?

   _____

   _____

   _____

   _____

   _____

Problem Solver

On November 2, 1929, the first international group of women pilots was formed at Curtiss Field. This made the Valley Stream Field the "Women's Cradle of Aviation." The number of members was 99. The organization was called the "Ninety-Nines." Amelia Earhart became its first president. Amelia Earhart is remembered as the first woman to cross the Atlantic Ocean alone in 1932. She is also remembered for her mysterious disappearance. A poem from the "Ninety-Nines" 30th anniversary program tells about the group.

> "They were girls who could not sit beside
> The hearth — and see go by
> The joy, the pride, the thrills that ride
> With rovers of the sky."

1. What does this poem say about the women who became aviators?

_____

_____

_____

_____

_____

2. Why were the "Ninety-Nines" considered pioneers?

_____

_____

_____

_____

_____

Map Builder

Understanding a Resource Map

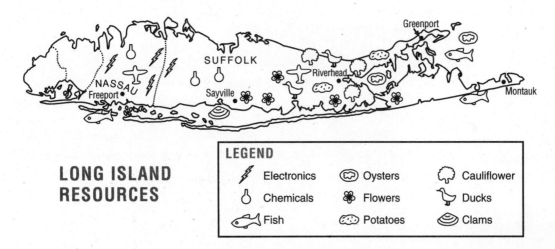

LONG ISLAND RESOURCES

LEGEND

⚡	Electronics	🦪	Oysters	🌳	Cauliflower
🧪	Chemicals	❀	Flowers	🦆	Ducks
🐟	Fish	🥔	Potatoes	🐚	Clams

Resource maps have pictures of things that are natural parts of the land, such as forests and minerals. They also show things people make or grow, such as airplanes and potatoes. They use symbols to represent products.

Look at the legend of the resource map above. There you see symbols for Long Island resources. For example, ❀ represents flowers. On the map, these symbols are placed where the resources are found, grown, or made.

1. Write a statement about the major resources of Long Island.

_____

_____

_____

2. Compare the resources of Nassau and Suffolk Counties.

_____

_____

_____

_____

CHAPTER 14

The People of Long Island

Before You Read

You have learned how farming and new business opportunities brought people to Long Island. Let's find out more about those people. What reasons do you think would make people leave the country where they were born to go to another country?

NEW TERMS

- immigrant
- Quakers
- Walt Whitman
- Theodore Roosevelt
- Sagamore Hill
- Gold Coast

Before 1830, there were mainly English and Dutch immigrants on Long Island. But after that, people of many different backgrounds came to the island. An *immigrant* is a person who leaves the country he or she was born in to live in a new country.

Immigrants from Many Countries

Immigrants came from France, Sweden, Norway, Germany, and Ireland. The French Huguenots came for religious freedom. The Swedish people hoped to find new jobs. The Germans were looking for more political

A Quaker meeting house

What do you think this building was used for?

freedom. In Ireland, a disease ruined the potato crop from 1845 to 1860. The food shortage forced people to leave the country to escape starvation.

Many black people from Africa were forced to come to America as slaves. Some farmers used slaves to do all the work on their farms.

A religious group known as the *Quakers* thought slavery was wrong. They fought against it. In 1827, slavery ended in New York state. The law set all Long Island slaves free 33 years before the Civil War. (Slavery ended even earlier in other northern states.)

In the late 1800s and early 1900s, more immigrants came. These immigrants came from Poland, Italy, Greece, Russia, and Romania. More recently, people from Puerto Rico, Spain, Latin America, Asia, Czechoslovakia, and India have joined the Long Island community.

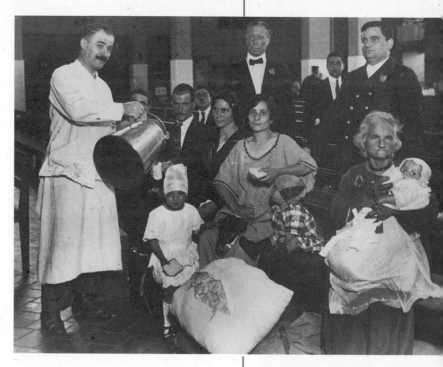

People from many nations immigrated to Long Island.

Why did they leave their native lands?

Long Island Counties

Long Island has steadily grown in population. In 1790, there were 36,949 people on the island. By 1890, that figure had grown to 1,029,097.

In 1980, the population of all four counties on Long Island was 6,908,000. At that time, more people lived in Nassau than in Suffolk County. However, population counts for 1990 indicated a change. Suffolk County had 1,321,864 residents, and Nassau had 1,287,348.

Up until 1898, Long Island consisted of three counties — Kings, Queens, and Suffolk. What we know as Nassau was once part of Queens County.

In 1898, Kings (Brooklyn) and a portion of Queens County became part of New York City. The rest of Queens County became the separate county of Nassau in 1899.

In this book we have thought of Long Island as a big fish made up of four counties. Politically speaking, Kings (Brooklyn) and Queens are part of New York City. These communities, however, are still closely connected to Long Island.

The Good Grey Poet

We have talked about the large groups of people who came to Long Island. There were also many individuals who made special contributions. Two of these were *Walt Whitman* (1819-1892) and *Theodore Roosevelt* (1858-1919).

Walt Whitman was a famous poet who was born in West Hills, Long Island, in 1819. He was known as "the Good Grey Poet" because of his long grey beard and good mood. Whitman's most well-known poems are collected in a book called *Leaves of Grass*. He wrote a number of poems about Long Island. One of these is called "Starting from Fish-Shaped Paumanok."

Walt Whitman

Why was he called "the Good Grey Poet"?

"T.R."

From 1901 to 1909, Theodore Roosevelt was the 26th President of the United States. He was also a Long Islander. In 1884, Roosevelt built a home in Oyster Bay called *Sagamore Hill*.

While Roosevelt was President, Sagamore Hill was known as the "summer White House." Today, this house is full of animal trophies and

Theodore Roosevelt

Why is he considered an important Long Islander?

Sagamore Hill

Does this look like your idea of a president's house? Why or why not?

books. It reflects the President's interests in history and the outdoors. Sagamore Hill is open to the public.

The Gold Coast

Because of its attractive location, Long Island became the home of many wealthy people. Beginning in the late 1800s, a series of estates was built on the North Shore of the island. These mansions stretched from Manhasset to Huntington. This area is called the "*Gold Coast.*"

F.W. Woolworth, J.P. Morgan, and William Vanderbilt built estates there. These men were successful industrial leaders who became millionaires.

Their large mansions were called the "castles of the wealthy." They had many floors, rooms, and special features. The houses were furnished with expensive furniture and art treasures from all over the world.

The grounds often had tennis courts, horse stables, and greenhouses. Many people were employed to keep these mansions running smoothly. Some of these estates have been turned into museums. Coe Hall at Planting Fields and Vanderbilt Mansion in Centerport are both open to the public.

Long Island's people have made and continue to make the island a special place to live and work.

CHAPTER review 14

Recalling What You Read

On the blank line, write **True** if the statement is correct.
If the statement is false, change the underlined word to
make it correct. Write the new word on the blank line.

1. An area of Long Island that features estates built
   by millionaires is called the <u>Playground</u>.   _____

2. In 1990, the population of Suffolk County was
   <u>larger</u> than that of Nassau County.   _____

3. A religious group that fought against slavery was
   called the <u>Quakers</u>.   _____

4. A famous Long Island poet was <u>J.P. Morgan</u>.   _____

5. In recent years, many people from <u>France</u> have
   immigrated to the United States.   _____

6. New York passed a law against owning slaves <u>after</u>
   the Civil War.   _____

7. <u>Suffolk</u> County was originally part of Queens County. _____

Think About It

1. The United States is said to be a "melting pot" of people. Explain how this is
   true about Long Island.

   _____

   _____

   _____

2. Tell what is meant by the Gold Coast. Describe what life was like in this area
   of Long Island.

   _____

   _____

   _____

124

Problem Solver

Walt Whitman wrote "Paumanok" near the end of his life. Below are a few lines of the poem. What is he saying about Long Island?

> "Sea beauty! stretch'd and basking!
> Isle of sweet brooks of drinking water — healthy air and soil!
> Isle of the salty shore and breeze and brine!"

1. What words help you to know Whitman's feeling about Long Island?

_____

_____

_____

_____

_____

_____

2. Do you agree with Whitman about Long Island? Why or why not?

_____

_____

_____

_____

_____

_____

14

Map Builder

Interpreting a Population Map

A population map tells you how many people live in an area. One type of population map is called a population density map. It shows how many people live in each acre or square mile of an area.

On a population map, dots can be used to represent people. If there are many dots close together, it means that many people live in that area. Fewer dots mean fewer people.

Some population maps show the number of people living in certain villages, towns, or cities. These maps use symbols to show the size of the population of each place.

Study the Long Island population map below. The symbols used to represent the population of the different areas are explained in the legend.

NASSAU AND SUFFOLK COUNTY POPULATION MAP

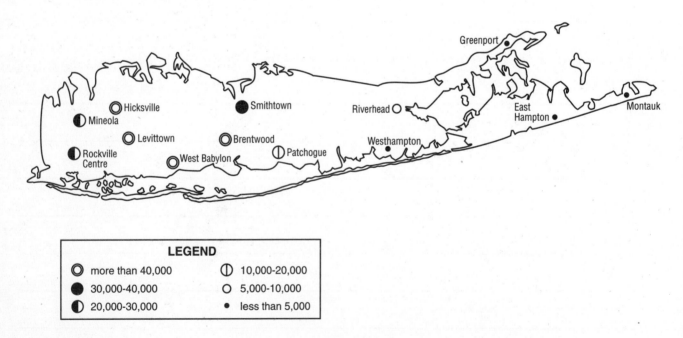

LEGEND

◎	more than 40,000	◐	10,000-20,000
●	30,000-40,000	○	5,000-10,000
◑	20,000-30,000	•	less than 5,000

Using the map on page 126, complete the following questions.

1. What conclusion can you make about the difference in population of towns in Nassau and Suffolk Counties?

_____

_____

_____

_____

_____

2. Explain why you think the towns on eastern Long Island have a smaller population than those on the west.

_____

_____

_____

_____

_____

True or False

Write a **T** next to each sentence that is true. Write an **F** next to each sentence that is false.

_____ **1.** Many parts of the whale were once valuable and useful.

_____ **2.** Today, the Long Island Railroad does very little business.

_____ **3.** Long Island workers helped win two world wars by building battleships and fighter planes.

_____ **4.** There is no place for farming on busy, industrial Long Island.

_____ **5.** MacArthur Airport is one of the world's largest airports.

_____ **6.** Commercial fishing is no longer important to Long Island.

LI Inquiry

1. All forms of transportation — water, land, and air — have been important to the development of Long Island. Support this statement giving specific examples of each.

_____

_____

_____

_____

2. Many individuals have been important to the development of Long Island. Choose three people whom you have read about and tell why they were important for Long Island.

_____

_____

_____

_____

_____

_____

Exploring Long Island

Project 4

How much information can you find about your community's early development? Was whaling important? How about farming? How did progress in transportation affect your area? What industries developed in the last century?

Divide up into groups. Each group will be responsible for gathering information. As a group, present your information to the class as an oral report.

Here are some sources of information for groups to contact:

1. Senior citizens who have lived in the community for many years

2. Old, established neighborhood businesses

3. Local museums

4. Historic sites of interest

5. Community libraries

6. Long Island Railroad offices

7. Large industrial plants

Long Island Today

The lighthouse at Montauk, one of Long Island's many tourist attractions.

CHAPTER 15 Industrial Development Since 1945

Before You Read

In this chapter, you will learn how Long Island's economy changed after World War II. What were some products made to help win the war?

*I*n 1945, World War II ended. Industries across the United States had been making products to help Americans win the war. Now they could return to peacetime activities. The same could be said for Long Island businesses.

Aircraft and Aerospace

The Grumman Corporation, for example, stopped building as many fighter planes. They had time for new projects such as the LEM.

The LEM is the *Lunar Excursion Module*. It was a vehicle used by American astronauts when they landed on the moon in 1969. Part of the LEM was left on the moon. Some people say it's like having a little bit of Long Island on the moon.

In 1994, the Grumman Corporation *merged* with the Northrop Company to become Northrop-Grumman. Until 1994, Grumman had been the largest employer on Long Island. After the merger, 28,000 people lost their jobs. In March 1997, there were only about 3,700 people working at Northrop-Grumman in Bethpage.

The Grumman corporation consented to the sale because they had been losing profits. Grumman was a small defense company when compared to other defense

companies in the United States. With the collapse of the Soviet empire, the United States government reduced its defense buying. Grumman could no longer compete with the bigger defense contractors. Northrop, a larger company, wanted Grumman's computers, so it offered to buy the company. Grumman accepted its offer. The new company makes electronic systems.

Besides Grumman, other Long Island firms developed peacetime aircraft and aerospace products for a while. Two of these firms were Sperry Rand (now Unisys) and Fairchild Republic.

The Lunar Excursion Module on the moon

What was the importance of the LEM?

Research Laboratories on Long Island

A former military camp became the headquarters of many scientists. *Brookhaven National Laboratory* was built on the old Camp Upton military site on eastern Long Island.

Brookhaven is run by a board of directors from nine northeastern universities. The laboratory employs more than 3,000 people. Many of these are scientists doing important atomic research. Their goal is to find peaceful ways to use atomic power.

These scientists also study the effects of pollution on the environment. Pollution is when air, water, and other substances become so dirty that they are harmful to living things.

Brookhaven worker and her seeing eye dog

On what might she be working?

A *Northrop-Grumman worker tests the Laser Measurement System*

How do you think her job has changed over the years?

The scientists are also concerned with the causes of disease and the safety of nuclear reactors. Brookhaven has a nuclear reactor. It is used to produce energy for experiments.

There are many other research laboratories on Long Island. The *Cold Spring Harbor Laboratory* is an internationally known research center for biology. *Biology* is the study of living things. Scientists from all over the world come to this famous laboratory. In 1983, the Nobel Prize for Medicine was awarded to Cold Spring Harbor scientist Barbara McClintock.

Tech Island

In the last ten years, Nassau and Suffolk counties have added thousands of new businesses. Some of these businesses are owned by foreign countries. Japan operates the most foreign-owned companies on the island.

Long Island has been called *Tech Island* because of the many firms that specialize in the manufacturing of technical equipment. This includes everything from computers to airplane parts.

Most of these firms are located in industrial parks. An *industrial park* is an area that is specially designed to contain a group of industries or businesses.

Why have the leaders of so many technical firms chosen to locate on Long Island? There are many skilled workers on the island. Costs are reasonable. Transportation is good. Employees can live and work in a nice area.

1995 LONG ISLAND BUSINESS ACTIVITY

Business Type	Number
Agricultural Services, Forestry, Fisheries	2,144
Mining (Sand & Gravel)	20
Construction	8,538
Manufacturing	4,164
Transportation & Public Utilities	3,075
Wholesale Trade	8,462
Retail Trade	17,814
Finance, Insurance, Real Estate	7,046
Services	31,661
Other	1,310
TOTAL	84,234

Source: NYS Department of Labor

Service Businesses

There are many other types of businesses on the island. Study the chart above. It lists all types of business activity recorded on Long Island in 1995.

Notice that "Services" is the largest category. Services are businesses that meet people's needs. Examples of businesses that provide services are hotels, laundromats, hair salons, photo-processing stores, auto repair centers, movie theaters, and even law firms.

Another large category is "Retail trade." *Retail trade* is the sale of goods to the general public. Long Island has many department and grocery stores. There are also many shops that specialize in one type of item, such as books or shoes.

Wholesale trade refers to the sale of goods in large quantities. This category is for businesses that sell to storekeepers. On Long Island, these places number more than 8,300.

Manufacturing

Manufacturing is the making of products in factories or shops. Clothing and textiles, chemicals, and paper products, are all manufactured on Long Island.

Notice that construction is an important business activity. In the last twenty years, many million-dollar projects have been completed. Libraries, hospitals, shopping malls, and hotels are just a few of these.

Since 1945, Long Island has seen much industrial growth. This growth has brought more people to live and work on the island. In the next chapter, you'll find out more about these people.

St. James General Store

What do you think they sell here?

135

Recalling What You Read

In the blank lines, write the word that best identifies each statement. When you have finished, the boxed letters will spell out the mystery word. Fill this word in at the end.

1. _ _ _ _ _ _ _ _ _ ☐ _ _ _   Workers in this Long Island business activity built hospitals and shopping malls.

2. _ _ _ _ ☐ _ _ _ _ _   The selling of homes is part of this Long Island business.

3. ☐ _ _ _ _ _ _ _ _ _ _ _ _ _ _ _ _ _   Scientists from all over the world come to this laboratory to learn about living things.

4. _ _ _ _ _ ☐ _ _ _ _ _ _ _ _ _ _ _ _ _   _ _ _ _ _ _ _ _ _ _ _   This is where scientists are looking for peaceful ways to use atomic power.

5. _ _ _ _ ☐ _ _ _   This type of business activity meets peoples' needs.

6. _ _ _ _ ☐ _ _ _ _   Grumman, Fairchild Republic, and Sperry Rand had helped to make Long Island a one-time leader in this industry.

7. ☐ _ _ _ _ _ _ _ _ _ _ _ _ _ _   _ _ _ _ _ _   Part of this was left on the moon when the first astronauts landed.

8. _ _ _ _ _ _ _ _ ☐ _ _ _ _ _   An area where many similar businesses are located near each other.

9. __ __ __ __ ☐   The most foreign-owned businesses on Long Island are operated by this country.

10. __ __ __ __ __ __   __ __ __ ☐ __   This business activity is the selling of goods to the general public.

Mystery Word __ __ __ __   __ __ __ __ __ __   Because of its many technical firms, Long Island has been given this nickname.

Think About It

1. Explain why many business owners have located to Long Island.

_____

_____

_____

_____

2. Study the chart on Long Island business activity on page 134. What does it tell you about the kind of people who live and work on Long Island?

_____

_____

_____

_____

Problem Solver

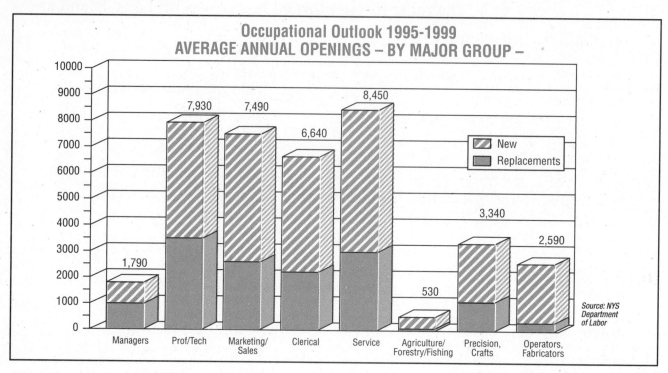

Occupational Outlook 1995-1999
AVERAGE ANNUAL OPENINGS – BY MAJOR GROUP –

New
Replacements

Managers 1,790
Prof/Tech 7,930
Marketing/Sales 7,490
Clerical 6,640
Service 8,450
Agriculture/Forestry/Fishing 530
Precision, Crafts 3,340
Operators, Fabricators 2,590

Source: NYS
Department
of Labor

1. Long Island has been called Tech Island. Based on what you've learned about Long Island industry, come up with another nickname and explain why it is appropriate.

_____

_____

_____

_____

2. Look at the bar graph of the Occupational Outlook for Long Island above. What conclusions can you make about the largest businesses on Long Island? Does the graph support the nickname Tech Island? Why or why not?

_____

_____

_____

_____

Map Builder

Drawing a Community Map

Here is a map of a section of the Seaford community. Understanding this map will prepare you for drawing a map of your own community.

Look carefully at this map and tell what important part is missing. Why is it important to have that on a map? What would you not be able to tell because it is missing?

_____

_____

_____

_____

_____

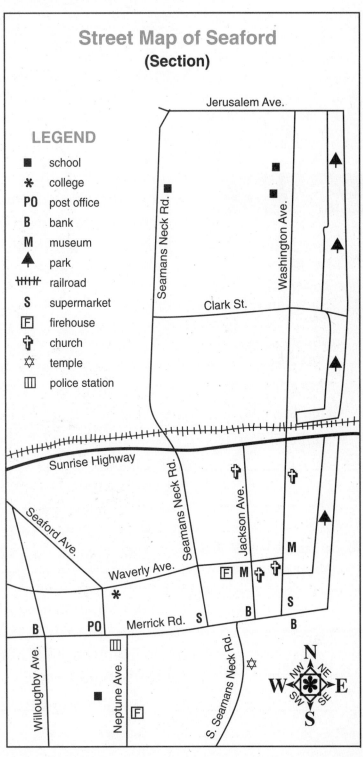

Next, create a map of your own community. First, locate the major roads in your community. Put them on the map and label them. Study the legend on the map on this page. If possible, add the things it shows to your own map.

In addition, decide what other landmarks you want to show. Make up symbols for each of these. Be sure your map has a legend and compass rose.

CHAPTER 16 Living and Working

Before You Read

This chapter explains why people moved to Long Island and where they went to live. Why did Long Island grow so quickly? Are there places left on Long Island for people to move to?

NEW TERMS

- consumer services
- Levittown
- suburbs
- white-collar workers
- blue-collar jobs
- Pine Barrens
- aquifer

*L*ong Island is considered a good place to live and work. Adequate housing is available. There is a wide variety of *consumer services*. This means that there are plenty of shopping areas, restaurants, banks, and pharmacies for the different communities.

The Development of Levittown

In its early history, much of Long Island was devoted to farming. After World War II, housing and industry took over a great deal of farmland.

During the 1940s, potatoes were an important crop on Long Island. Worms destroyed that crop. Many farmers in Nassau County stopped growing potatoes, and their land became available for other uses.

About the same time, large numbers of soldiers returned home from World War II. They needed houses to live in. A man named Abraham Levitt wanted to supply those homes.

With his sons as partners, Levitt bought large amounts of land from former potato farmers. Most of this land was in the Hempstead Plains area. In 1947, Levitt and Sons began building homes on this land. This was the start of what became known as *Levittown*.

Levittown is a large development of affordable homes. Each section of the development has its own schools, shopping center, and recreational area. The houses are very similar to each other. By 1951, there were more than 17,000 new homes in this area.

The Growth of Suburbs

Home building continued to increase on Long Island. Housing developments spread to Suffolk County. Modern highways and a good railroad system made it possible for people to live further and further out on the island. They could get to their jobs in New York City by riding the commuter trains.

Levittown in the 1950s

How do you think it has changed?

Large areas outside a city where many people live are called *suburbs*. Since World War II, suburban living has become a popular American lifestyle. By the early 1970s, more Americans lived in suburbs than in large cities.

There were many reasons for this. People wanted to get away from crowded city conditions. They felt suburban living meant better education and other opportunities for their families.

There is a high regard for education on Long Island. The island has 22 colleges and universities. Each community has established its own school system.

More people meant the creation of more businesses to meet their needs. It also meant more jobs for Long Islanders.

The Building of Shopping Malls

People living in the suburbs didn't want to travel into the city every time they needed to buy something. Small businesses were started to meet suburban needs. The industries you read about in Chapter 15 were established. Modern shopping malls were built.

A shopping mall has something for everyone. There are department stores, specialty shops, and food services. These are all combined into one large area with convenient parking. Most malls are enclosed. This means you can walk from store to store without going outside.

One popular Long Island mall is Roosevelt Field in Garden City. It is one of the nation's largest malls. Sunrise Mall in Massapequa is another popular mall. South Shore Mall in Bay Shore, with more than 100 stores, attracts many customers.

The Roosevelt Field Mall in Garden City

Why do so many people shop here?

New Businesses on Long Island

Thousands of Long Islanders work at jobs in New York City. There is also plenty of opportunity for employment

LONG ISLAND'S LARGEST EMPLOYERS, 1995

Rank	Company	Employees on LI
1.	Diocese of Rockville Centre	12,500
2.	North Shore Health System	11,002
3.	Waldbaum's	6,500
4.	Long Island Railroad	6,068
5.	Long Island Lighting Company	5,947
6.	LI Jewish Medical Center	5,880
7.	Northrop-Grumman	5,000
8.	Chemical Banking	4,500
9.	King Kullen	4,500
10.	NYNEX	4,500

Source: 1996 Long Island Almanac

on the island itself. Study the chart on page 142. It lists ten of Long Island's largest employers.

The Catholic Church's Diocese at Rockville Center led the 1995 list with 12,500 employees. Public utilities such as Long Island Lighting Company and NYNEX also provide many jobs.

Most of Long Island's labor force are *white-collar workers*. These are people who work in offices. Managers and secretaries are examples of this. Professional people such as lawyers and teachers are also white-collar workers.

A smaller number of Long Island's workers have *blue-collar jobs*. This means that they have non-office occupations. Examples of this include factory employees and bus drivers.

How do people find out what jobs are available on Long Island? One way is to read the classified ads in *Newsday*. With more than 700,000 readers, *Newsday* is an important daily newspaper on Long Island. It was started in 1940 in Garden City and is now published in Melville.

Office workers
What kind of work could they be doing?

A sheet metal worker
What other Long Island industries benefit from his labor?

143

In addition to *Newsday*, there are more than 100 community weekly newspapers serving Long Island readers. These smaller papers keep people informed of local events.

The Pine Barrens

Long Island offers its many residents a wide variety of jobs and places to live.

However, there is a part of Long Island that cannot be developed by new population, housing, or business. It is in Suffolk County. This area is called the *Pine Barrens*. The pine barrens are low growing pine trees that are on top of a layer of soil and rock that retains water. This underground layer is called an *aquifer*. The county government has a law that protects the Pine Barrens from development. A fund was established to maintain the Pine Barrens. The Pine Barrens protect Long Island's drinking water.

Modern-day commuters return from New York City

Go back and look at the picture on page 107. What has changed?

Recalling What You Read
Complete the following sentences by filling in the blanks.

1. People who work in factories are known as _____ workers.

2. The place that employed the most people on Long Island in 1995 was

    _____ .

3. The first large housing development on Long Island was built by

    _____ .

4. An enclosed shopping area that has many types of stores is called a

    _____ .

5. People who work in offices are called _____ workers.

6. The daily newspaper on Long Island is _____ .

7. An area outside a city where people live is called a _____ .

Think About It

1. What do you think are the advantages and disadvantages of living in a suburb?

    _____

    _____

    _____

    _____

2. Explain why your family lives on Long Island.

    _____

    _____

    _____

    _____

Problem Solver

Abraham Levitt, the builder of Levittown, said that he wanted his company to "build neighborhoods, not houses." *Time* magazine ran an article about Levittown in 1950. The slogan on its cover was: "For Sale: A New Way of Life."

In addition to houses, the Levitts built village greens, swimming pools, playgrounds, a baseball field, and a $250,000 community center.

1. What did Abraham Levitt mean when he said he wanted to create a neighborhood?

_____

_____

_____

2. What is a "way of life"? How was it created in Levittown? Do you think this was a good idea? Why or why not?

_____

_____

_____

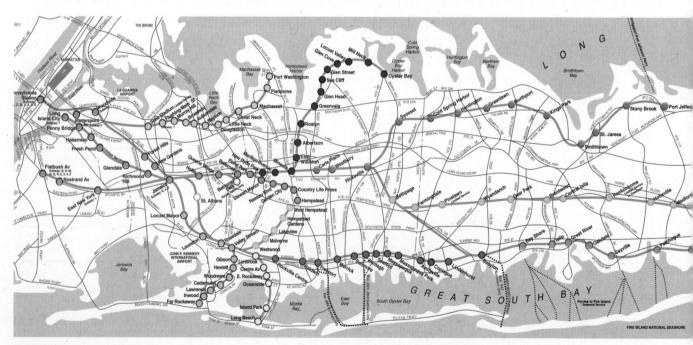

Map Builder 16

Long Island Rail Road Routes

Study the map below. As you can see there is more than one railroad that goes from Long Island into New York City.

1. Explain why you think there are different railroad lines.

_____

_____

_____

2. Which line of the railroad do you think carries the most passengers? Why?

_____

_____

3. What would you have to do to travel from Babylon to Huntington by railroad?

_____

_____

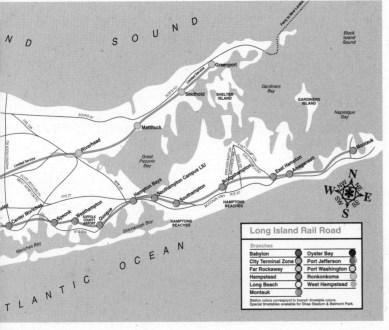

4. Would the railroad be the best way to travel between these two places? Why or why not?

_____

_____

_____

_____

_____

_____

CHAPTER 17 Recreation

Before You Read

Do you like the beach? What about a nature trail? This chapter will tell you about the places where you can have fun on Long Island.

NEW TERMS

- nor'easter
- sanctuary

*W*hat's your idea of a good vacation? Do you like to swim at the beach? Are you interested in sports? Do you enjoy observing wildlife? Whatever you're interested in, you don't need to travel far to find it on Long Island.

The South Shore Beaches

There are more than 1,000 miles of shoreline on the island. On the South Shore, beaches extend from Sea Gate in Brooklyn to Montauk Point in Suffolk. Millions of island residents and visitors flock to the South Shore each year. There they enjoy swimming, boating, surfing, and other water sports.

Jones Beach

In what ways are these people using the resources of Long Island?

Long Island's shoreline is undergoing continual change. *Erosion* on the barrier beaches just off the South Shore occurs during hurricane season from September to November. Major erosion also takes place during fall and winter storms, especially during a *"nor'easter,"* which is a storm with strong winds coming from the northeast. Erosion is a loss of beach front caused by sand being washed away by wave and storm action. People's homes on a barrier beach called Fire Island have actually been washed into the sea and destroyed. Erosion is also a problem on the North Shore because the high cliffs become weak. All of this activity may reduce the enjoyment of Long Island beaches in the future.

Erosion forces a house to close up.

How does this kind of activity impact the tourism and recreation industry?

One of Long Island's most famous recreational areas is Jones Beach. This well-known resort was designed by Robert Moses in 1924. Part of Moses' design was to build parkways that took travelers directly to Jones Beach.

Sports on Long Island

Sports of all kinds are popular with Long Island residents and vacationers. There are 95 year-round tennis clubs and hundreds of public courts. A world-famous tennis tournament, the U.S. Open, is held yearly at the National Tennis Center in Flushing Meadow, Queens. Golf is also popular. There is also a U.S. Open in golf. It is one of the major tournaments on the PGA Tour. It was held at Shinnecock Hills in 1986 and 1995. There are over 100 golf courses on the island.

Sailboat racing is another favorite Long Island pastime. There are over 400 marinas and yacht clubs on the island. Also, sport fishing attracts many visitors.

Corey Pavin wins the 1995 U.S. Open at Shinnecock Hills.

What makes Long Island a good place for a major golf tournament?

The New York Islanders

How does a "hometown" team bring a community together?

Spectator sports are very important to Long Islanders. One such sport is horse racing. Aqueduct racetrack is in Queens. Belmont Park is in Nassau.

Other spectator sports Long Islanders actively support are baseball, football, and hockey. Baseball fans can cheer the New York Mets at Shea Stadium in Queens. Football enthusiasts root for the New York Jets at their training camp at Hofstra University in Hempstead. Hockey fans applaud the Islanders at Nassau Veterans Memorial Coliseum. In recent years, indoor lacrosse and monster truck competitions have also become popular.

Parklands to Visit

Nature lovers find much to appreciate on Long Island. There are 55,000 acres of parkland. These parks are filled with things to do. You can picnic or participate in sports. You can stroll through gardens or down a nature trail.

In the summer, musicians give outdoor concerts. You can also visit historic places of interest such as the Walt Whitman House in Huntington. You can watch for unusual birds in wildlife sanctuaries. A *sanctuary* is a place where animals and birds live and are protected.

Long Island offers many recreational activities for vacationers and island residents.

A picnic at Planting Fields Arboretum in Oyster Bay

What are some of the other things you can do here?

Recalling What You Read

Here are some ways to have fun on Long Island.
In the blanks, write one location for each activity.
Use information only from this chapter.

1. watch a horse race _____

2. go to a Mets game _____

3. see the Islanders play _____

4. swim in the ocean _____

Think About It

1. Prove the following statement. There are recreational activities for everyone on Long Island.

_____

_____

_____

_____

_____

2. How was Robert Moses important to recreational activities on Long Island?

_____

_____

_____

_____

Problem Solver

In Chapter 10, you learned the important role of whaling in Long Island history. Whale watches are a popular pastime today. The following is a passage from a federal guide to recreation on Long Island.

"The Okeanos whale watch/research vessel, the Viking Starship, is a fast, comfortable 140-foot steel vessel that offers a full galley/gift shop, large heated cabin seating over 220 passengers, observation sun-deck with seating for over 100 passengers, television/video system, and public address system for easy listening to a naturalist's lecture."

1. How are whale watches today different from the whale watches in the 1700s and 1800s?

   _____

   _____

   _____

   _____

   _____

2. What does this say about Long Island today compared to Long Island of the 1700s and 1800s?

   _____

   _____

   _____

   _____

   _____

Map Builder

Using a Pictorial Map

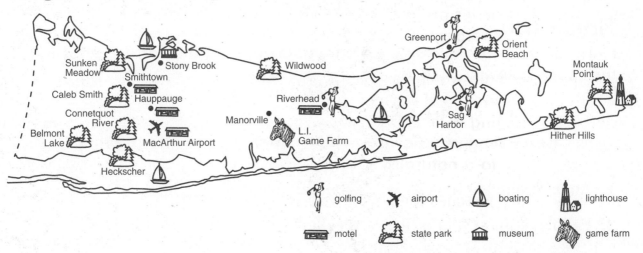

A pictorial map shows places of interest. It can help you find recreation spots, such as golf courses and stadiums. It can also include museums and historical sites. Some pictorial maps even show hotels, restaurants, and airports.

Instead of dots or squares, a pictorial map uses small pictures. For example, a state park on the map above looks like 🏞️.

Look at the map on this page. Write a letter to a friend who doesn't live on Long Island. Invite him/her to come to Long Island. Tell your friend the different places you will be able to go to and the things that you will be able to do.

Dear_____ ,

_____

_____

_____

_____

_____

_____

Your Friend, _____

Finish Up

Finish each of the following statements by putting the correct letter in the space below.

a – service industry   b – suburb

c – ice hockey   d – white collar   e – Tech Island

1. An area outside the city where people live is a _____ .

2. People employed in offices are called _____ workers.

3. Because of its many technical companies, Long Island has been nicknamed _____ .

4. The largest number of businesses on Long Island are in the _____ .

5. A popular spectator sport on the island is _____ .

LI Inquiry

1. You have been chosen to write a column for a magazine to encourage people to move to Long Island. Write your column, making sure you include the types of jobs available, transportation, recreation, shopping, and all other reasons someone would want to live on Long Island.

_____

_____

_____

_____

_____

_____

_____

2. "Suffolk County is becoming more and more like Nassau County." Explain whether or not you agree with this statement. Include at least five specific examples to support your argument.

_____

_____

_____

_____

_____

_____

_____

Exploring Long Island

Project 5

Charting Your Community's Business Development

What businesses and industries are located in your community? How can you find out more about them? Here are some suggestions:

1. Plan a field trip to the business section.

2. Invite a community business leader to speak to the class. The Lions Club or local Rotary could help you find a speaker.

3. Visit a real estate office. Ask about buying homes in your area.

4. Study the classified advertising section of the newspaper. It will show you what jobs are offered in your area.

5. Visit the local chamber of commerce. Someone there can tell you how the tourist industry has helped business in your town.

With this information, create your own chart on types and numbers of businesses in your community.

UNIT 6 Local Government

A group of Long Island politicians

Before You Read

Do you live in an incorporated village? Would you like to? This chapter will explain how government works at the village level.

*I*magine yourself in a country with no government. There would be no laws or rules to follow. Roads and traffic lights wouldn't exist. Police officers would not be there to protect you. What else would be missing?

The Federal Government

Luckily, you don't have to live this way. In the United States, we have a *democratic* government. This means that the people decide how the country should be run. This is done by electing government leaders to represent us.

The *federal government*, located in Washington, D.C., makes laws that affect every person in the United States. But America is a very large country. The federal government can't make and enforce every law for all fifty states.

Divisions of Government

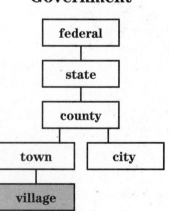

The State Government

For this reason, each state has its own separate government. Elected leaders in the *state government* make and enforce laws for their individual states.

You live in New York State. Your state government is located in Albany, New York.

Like the federal government, the state government can't handle everyone's needs. Because of this, there are local county governments. In addition to the county governments there are also village, town, and city governments. Each division has elected officials. Each division has special jobs to do.

The Village

We will begin with the village. This is the smallest unit of local government. You may, in fact, live in an *incorporated village*. Let's find out what that means.

As Long Island's population grew, people wanted more control over their town governments. They needed special services in their own areas. To get these services, they formed villages. A village is a smaller unit of government within a town.

One town may contain many villages. A village can be no bigger than three square miles. A village is made up of a group of concerned property owners. These people are willing to pay extra taxes to get special services.

Patchogue Village Hall

What kinds of activities go on here?

To become a village, the property owners meet together and sign a *petition*. This is a special paper that requests that their area be allowed to become a village. At least half of the property owners in the area must sign this petition.

The signed petition is brought to the town government. If this group votes "yes" on the petition, the proposed village is created. It is called an *incorporated village*.

Hamlets

Long Island has many places that seem like villages, because they are small areas with their own name. However, the people in the area haven't signed the petition that requests that their area become a village. These places are called *hamlets*. Hamlets don't have their own government but are part of the town government. Wading River and West Babylon are hamlets.

Village Government

The top elected official of an incorporated village is the *mayor*. A small group, called the *board of trustees*, helps the mayor run things. The mayor and the board make and enforce laws for the village. These officials are elected to office by the people of the village.

Each year, the mayor prepares a *budget*. It shows how the mayor thinks village tax money should be spent. The board of trustees may change this budget before approving it.

After approval, the board decides how much each person in the village should pay in taxes. This is called a *tax rate*. The board then supervises the collection of these taxes. This tax money is used to create special services for the people of the village.

What are these special services? Village governments provide water, sewage disposal, garbage removal, and road improvements. Villages have their own fire departments and recreation centers. Some villages have police protection.

Village government gives the people on Long Island more control over the rules in their local area.

A woman votes in a local election

What kinds of issues do you think she is considering?

Recalling What You Read

Use the words in the dark print to complete the following paragraphs. Write the letters you chose in the correct blanks.

a – taxes   **b – elected**   **c – mayor**   **d – budget**

e – special services   **f – money**   **g – board of trustees**

1. The chief officer of a village is the _____.

2. The small group that helps the mayor is the _____.

3. Both the mayor and this group are_____ by the people of the village.

4. One of the mayor's jobs is to prepare a _____.

5. It shows how the _____ will be spent.

6. The _____ are used to provide services for the people of the village.

Think About It

1. List the steps that have to be followed to become an incorporated village. What are the advantages and disadvantages of being an incorporated village?

   _____

   _____

   _____

   _____

2. What are some special services that a village government can provide?

   _____

   _____

   _____

   _____

Problem Solver

The federal government in Washington, D.C., is given power to do many things. The state government also has powers to do things that affect their individual states. Look at the list below. Which powers do you think should belong to the state governments? Which powers do you think should belong to the federal government? Why?

1. Grant marriage licenses _____

   _____

2. Train an army _____

   _____

3. Define crimes and their punishment _____

   _____

4. Determine the requirements for voting _____

   _____

5. Provide for public health _____

   _____

6. Build schools _____

   _____

7. Operate a post office _____

   _____

Map Builder

Political Map

A political map shows political boundaries. These are man-made boundaries as opposed to natural boundaries. This map shows the different voting districts for the Nassau County government.

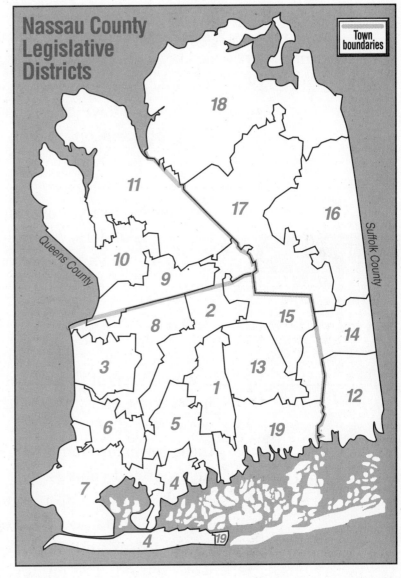

1. Describe two natural boundaries of Long Island.

2. Why do you think the legislative areas are not all equal in size?

_____

_____

_____

_____

_____

_____

CHAPTER 19 Town Government

Before You Read

Who fixes the roads in your town? What happens when snow needs to be removed? This chapter will explain how the town government works and how it affects the people on Long Island.

NEW TERMS

- town board
- town supervisor
- school district

*Y*ou have learned how important incorporated villages are to Long Islanders. A larger, even more important part of local government is the town government.

Town Meetings

Long Island is divided into 13 towns. Three of these towns are in Nassau County. Ten of them are in Suffolk County. Within these towns are many incorporated villages.

Look at the map on this page. It shows you the Long Island towns and the dates they were settled. The eight towns

Divisions of Government

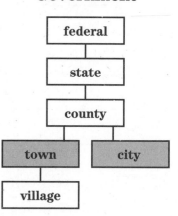

LONG ISLAND TOWNS WITH SETTLEMENT DATES

Newtown 1640
Flushing 1645
1644 North Hempstead
Oyster Bay 1653
Huntington 1653
Smithtown 1650
Brookhaven 1651
Riverhead 1640
Southold 1640
Shelter Island 1652
Brooklyn 1638
Flatbush 1651
Jamaica 1655
Hempstead 1644
Babylon 1653
Islip 1683
South Hampton 1640
PECONIC BAY
East Hampton 1648
New Utrecht 1654
Flatland 1636
Gravesend 1643

west of Hempstead and North Hempstead are now part of New York City.

Town meetings were very important to the early settlers. These meetings gave them a chance to make rules and choose their own leaders. The colonists were able to practice self-government.

Holding town meetings was a democratic way to run things. Many Long Islanders fought in the American Revolution so they could keep their self-government.

In the early days, all male property owners 21 years or older could take part in the town meetings. Today, too many people live in the towns for all of them to attend town meetings. Instead, there is a *town board* that represents the men and women of a town.

The Town Board

The town board has anywhere from four to eight members. The chairperson of the board is called the *town supervisor*. The other members of the board are called town councilmen or councilwomen. These local officials are elected by the voters in a town for either two- or four-year terms.

The supervisor is the chief official of the town. This person runs board meetings. He or she has many duties. One of these is to handle the town budget.

Town board meeting

What kinds of issues could they be addressing?

The supervisor estimates how much money is needed to run the town. He or she also suggests how to collect this money. The supervisor's recommendations are approved or changed by the town board.

The town board meets each week to discuss local issues. The board passes laws to protect the people of the town and to provide services for them.

The board grants permits or permission to build houses and factories. Roads, street lights, and traffic signs are under the board's control.

The board may appoint officials to carry out and run the town's business. In some places these officials are elected to the board. The chart that follows lists these officials and their jobs.

Town Official	Responsibilities
Town Clerk	• Keeps written records • Takes minutes at board meetings • Issues marriage, fishing licenses
Receiver of Taxes	• Collects taxes from townspeople
Assessor	• Decides value of property for tax purposes
Town Comptroller	• Oversees spending of town money
Superintendent of Highways	• Repairs and maintains roads
Town Engineer	• Handles building or construction
Town Attorney	• Looks out for legal matters

There are also departments within the town government that take care of special services. Some of these departments are parks and recreation, traffic control, and animal shelter and control. Other departments handle housing, industrial development, conservation, water, and safety.

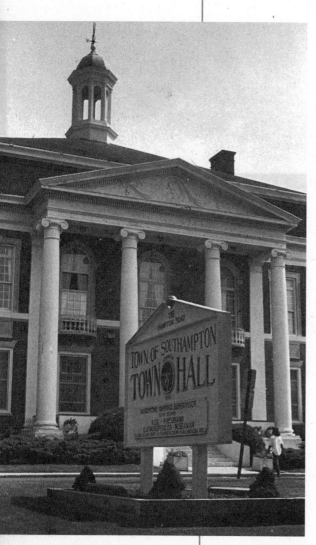

Southampton Town Hall

How does this Town Hall look different from the Village Hall on page 159?

Education on Long Island

Education is very important on Long Island. Each town has one or more *school districts*. How many districts a town has depends on the size of the town. Some towns on Long Island have as many as twenty school districts. Each school district is given its own number.

The people of each school district have a voice in running their schools. They vote on the school budget. They also elect members of a board of education. This board supervises the local school system.

City Government

You now know about the village and town government of Long Island. There is another form of local leadership called city government. Long Island has two cities — Glen Cove and Long Beach. Both are in Nassau County.

Town and city governments have no control over each other. Each has its own laws and special services. The highest officials in a city are the mayor and the city council.

Ever since colonial days, local government has been very important to the people of Long Island.

A policeman walking his beat in Patchogue Village

What kinds of problems do you think he encounters in a typical day?

Recalling What You Read

On the line to the left, write the name of the town official described below.

_____ **1.** collects the taxes

_____ **2.** keeps the records

_____ **3.** handles new construction

_____ **4.** checks legal matters

_____ **5.** watches how money is spent

Think About It

1. Explain why we don't make rules at town meetings today.

_____

_____

_____

_____

_____

2. Explain why there are so many different school districts. Do you think it would be better to combine school districts? Why or why not?

_____

_____

_____

_____

_____

Problem Solver

Study the following chart. It contains information on the population of Nassau County towns from 1950 to 1990. (Note: The populations of cities of Glen Cove and Long Beach have not been listed here.)

Census Year	Nassau County	Hempstead Town	No. Hempstead Town	Oyster Bay Town
1950	672,765	432,596	142,613	66,930
1960	1,300,171	740,738	219,088	290,055
1970	1,428,838	801,592	235,007	333,342
1980	1,321,582	738,517	218,624	305,750
1990	1,287,348	725,639	211,393	292,657
2000	_____	_____	_____	_____

1. What happened to the population of the towns from 1950 to 1960? Why do you think that happened? What happened to the population between between 1970 and 1990? Why do you think that is happening?

_____

_____

_____

_____

_____

2. Fill in the populations for the year 2000. Explain your answers.

_____

_____

_____

_____

Map Builder

19

Reviewing Your Map Skills 1

You have learned how to read many different types of maps. Let's review and test that skill. Study the map below and then complete the statements that follow. The map shows Nassau and Suffolk counties. You will only be answering questions about your own county.

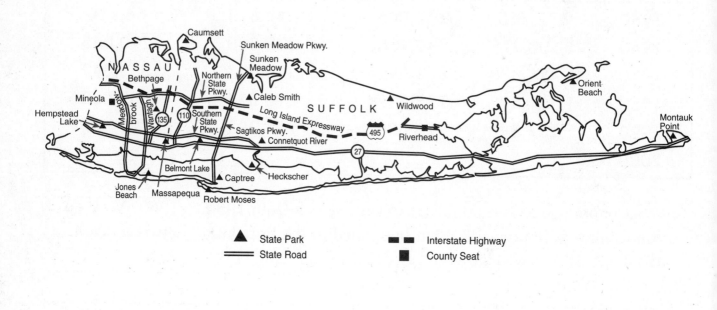

FACTS ABOUT _____ COUNTY

1. The county seat is located at _____ .

2. There are _____ state parks located in my county. Two of them are

_____ and

_____ .

3. The interstate highway that runs through my county is _____ .

4. My county's width is (close to, not close to) its length. Circle the best answer.

5. If I wanted to travel east and west through the middle of my county, I would use

_____ .

6. A road I could travel north and south on in my county is

_____ .

7. Tell two things that this map does not tell you about Long Island.

_____

_____

_____

_____

8. What other symbols could you add to this map? Do you think those symbols would make this a better map?

_____

_____

_____

_____

_____

_____

CHAPTER 20 County Government

Before You Read

County government is the most important division of Long Island local government. How is a county different from a state? From a hamlet? From a village?

*Y*ou have now seen how government operates in the villages and towns of Long Island. Let's take a look at the way the county government is run.

The Services of the County

The county provides Long Island residents with many extra services. It pays for things the town and village governments can't afford. The county government carries out many state laws and regulations. For example, county officials make sure people obey state traffic laws. They maintain health standards that have been decided upon by the state government.

Divisions of Government

```
          federal
             |
           state
             |
          county
          /      \
       town       city
         |
      village
```

As you know from reading this book, Long Island now has two independent counties: Nassau and Suffolk. Originally, Long Island was divided into three counties: Kings (Brooklyn), Queens, and Suffolk. These three counties were established by the Duke of York in 1683.

In 1898, Kings (Brooklyn) and a section of Queens became part of New York City. The other part of Queens was renamed Nassau County.

NEW TERMS

- county executive
- legislature
- district attorney
- county clerk
- county comptroller
- county medical examiner
- social services
- planning commission
- board of elections
- civil service commission

Working on Suffolk
County roads

*Why would
the county be
responsible
for maintaining
the roads?*

From earlier map work, you may remember that Mineola is the center of county government for Nassau. For Suffolk, the county seat is Riverhead.

County Government Leaders

Let's find out how these county governments are organized. The head elected official is called the *county executive*. This person is in office for four years. Preparing the budget is the county executive's biggest responsibility. This highest official also serves on the county *legislature*.

The legislative body is a group of men and women who make the laws for the county. They are elected by the voters of the county and meet once a week. These lawmakers are called *legislators*. Nassau County has 19 legislators and Suffolk County has 18. The legislatures represent different sections of the county.

The Suffolk County Legislature came into being in 1970. The Nassau County Legislature had its first meeting in February 1996. Before this meeting, Nassau County government consisted of a board of six supervisors with a county executive. Nassau County had this form of government since it became a county in 1899.

A member is sworn into the Nassau County Legislature.

Do you think the new legislature represents all the people of the county?

The Board of Supervisors represented Nassau's three towns — Hempstead, North Hempstead, and Oyster Bay — and two cities, Glen Cove and Long Beach. The problem was that Hempstead had two of the six supervisors. The other towns and cities had only one. This system of government was deemed to be unfair by the Supreme Court of the United States because one town — Hempstead — could control many decisions.

Today there is a legislature with 19 members, each representing a district of about 70,000 members. The new system better represents local communities. A committee system can now look over bills and decide which ones should be considered. There is also a presiding officer chosen by the legislature in order to direct discussion at the meetings. The county executive does not meet with the legislature.

County Officials

Besides these people, there are other officials that help run county government. The chart below describes their jobs and the duties involved.

COUNTY OFFICIALS

Job Title	Responsibilities
County Clerk	• Keeps track of official records— property deeds, land maps, etc.
County Comptroller	• Watches out for county's money • Okays payments of county money
District Attorney	• Prosecutes lawbreakers • Proves guilt of criminals
County Medical Examiner	• Investigates suspicious deaths • Examines murder, suicide victims

In addition to these officials, there are a number of departments in the county government. The chart that follows shows these departments and the services they provide.

COUNTY DEPARTMENTS

Department	Services
Police	• Directs traffic • Keeps law and order • Protects people
Health	• Controls spread of disease • Supervises water purity • Checks sanitary conditions in restaurants
Social Services	• Finds homes for needy children • Takes care of homeless and elderly • Helps physically, mentally handicapped
Parks and Recreation	• Runs and maintains parks
Public Works	• Builds bridges, sewers, public buildings
Planning Commission	• Recommends changes for county growth
Board of Elections	• Holds and supervises elections
Civil Service Commission	• Oversees hiring of county employees

The Judicial Branch

The county government also has a judicial branch. This is the section of the government that enforces the laws. There are a number of courts where justice is upheld.

Those accused of breaking the law appear before the county judge. The judge or jury decides if the person is guilty of the accused crime.

There are several different types of courts in each county. There is the county court. Then there is the district court. The district court tries cases that are not as serious as the ones seen in the county court. Cases involving up to $6,000 worth of damage are tried in the district court.

More serious cases involving a jury trial take place in the supreme court. Murder cases are tried there.

In all divisions of Long Island's local government, the people have a chance to take an active part.

Recalling What You Read

On the line to the left, write the name of the official or the department identified.

_____ **1.** protects people

_____ **2.** holds elections

_____ **3.** helps needy people

_____ **4.** checks food and water conditions

_____ **5.** gathers evidence for trial

_____ **6.** supervises bridge building

_____ **7.** runs the county parks

_____ **8.** keeps track of official records

Think About It

1. Describe how county government helps to carry out the state laws.

_____

_____

_____

_____

2. Discuss the different types of courts in the county.

_____

_____

_____

_____

Problem Solver

Newsday had an article on the first historic meeting of the Nassau County legislature. The article helps us to understand why the county government was changed. Answer the questions after reading this part of the article below.

"Just minutes after taking their historic oath yesterday as the first African-Americans elected to county offices on Long Island, Darlene Harris and Roger Corbin spotted each other... 'A great duty has been laid in my lap,' said Harris, of Uniondale. She felt honored to be the first black woman elected to the legislature. Corbin added, 'Finally, we have some say in a county government that has totally left us out.'"

(from *Newsday* - February 12, 1996)

1. Why was the meeting of the Nassau County Legislature historic?

_____

_____

_____

_____

2. Why were blacks and other minorities not represented on the Board of Supervisors?

_____

_____

_____

_____

3. Why is it possible for minorities to be represented in the new government?

_____

_____

_____

Map Builder

Reviewing Your Map Skills 2

You have learned about many different types of maps. Now let's see if you can put all this knowledge together. Draw a map that shows the location of your home and school.

1. Explain step by step what you did to make this map and tell what you included on the map.

_____

_____

_____

_____

_____

_____

_____

_____

_____

_____

_____

_____

_____

_____

_____

178

Following the directions on page 178, create a map.

Map of My Home

Identify It

Read each of the following statements. Write a **V** if it is about village government. Put a **T** if it is about town government. Place a **C** if it is about county government. Write an **A** if the statement is true about all three levels of local government.

_____ **1.** has a chief elected official

_____ **2.** provides police protection

_____ **3.** collects taxes

_____ **4.** has mayor as chief official

_____ **5.** gives permission to build homes and factories

_____ **6.** issues marriage and fishing licenses

_____ **7.** holds restaurant inspections

_____ **8.** has supervisor as chief official

LI Inquiry

1. Do you think it is necessary to have village, town, and county governments? Why or why not?

_____

_____

_____

_____

_____

2. County government is the most important division of Long Island local government. Prove or disprove this statement.

_____

_____

_____

_____

_____

Exploring Long Island

Project 6

Create Your Own Town Government

Is there a law that you would like to see your local government pass?

Turn your classroom into a model town government. Elect one person to the role of town supervisor. Other people in class can be members of the town board. You will also need private citizens to debate the proposed new law.

Now role-play the process of getting the law passed. Go through the following steps:

1. Hold a classroom discussion to decide what law you would like passed. Brainstorm for ideas.

2. Write up the proposed new law as it would appear as a notice in the newspaper. Include the announcement of a public hearing.

3. Hold the hearing. Class members playing private citizens will debate the proposed new law. The supervisor and board members may ask them questions.

4. Have a simulated town council meeting. Vote on the proposal.

Chronology

Date	Event
1498	John Cabot sails to Long Island.
1524	Giovanni da Verrazano enters New York Bay.
1609	Henry Hudson sails to Long Island.
1614	Adrian Block proves that Long Island is an island.
1636	Dutch settle Long Island.
1639	Lion Gardiner buys an island.
1640	John Youngs founds Southold. The English settle Southampton.
1650	English and Dutch divide Long Island.
1664	Dutch surrender to English.
1665	The Duke's Laws are announced.
1683	Kings, Queens, Suffolk Counties are established.
1765	British Stamp Act is passed.
1772	Stagecoach service opens on Long Island.
1773	Americans hold Boston Tea Party.
1776	Long Islanders sign Declaration of Independence.
1783	Treaty of Paris is signed.
1790	President George Washington tours Long Island.
1796	Montauk Lighthouse is built.
1806	First turnpike is built on Long Island.
1819	Walt Whitman is born in West Hills.
1844	Long Island Railroad completes route to Boston.
1859	Discovery of petroleum oil hurts whaling.
1861	Civil War begins.
1862	*Monitor* is built in Brooklyn Navy Yard.
1865	Civil War ends.
1873	White Pekin duck industry begins on Long Island.

1883	Brooklyn Bridge is completed.
1898	Brooklyn Navy Yard builds the *Maine*. Brooklyn and Queens become part of New York City.
1899	Nassau County is created.
1908	First concrete highway is built on Long Island.
1909	Glen Curtiss makes solo flight.
1914	United States enters World War I.
1918	World War I ends.
1920	Robert Moses builds Long Island highway system.
1924	Robert Moses designs Jones Beach.
1927	Charles A. Lindbergh flies nonstop to Paris.
1939	World War II begins.
1940	*Newsday* begins operation.
1947	World War II ends. The start of Levittown.
1947	Brookhaven National Laboratory is built.
1951	Levittown expands to 17,000 new homes.
1969	LEM lands on the moon.
1980	New York Islanders win the first of four straight Stanley Cups.
1983	Nobel Prize for Science awarded to Cold Spring Harbor Laboratory scientist Barbara McClintock.
1994	Grumman Aerospace acquired by Northrop.
1994	Nassau County voters approve new legislature.
1996	Nassau County legislature meets for the first time.

Glossary

Algonquians – a group of Native Americans who lived along the east coast of North America, including Long Island

American Revolution – the war between America and Britain that was fought for American independence from 1776 to 1783

ambergris – a fluid from a whale's intestines used to make perfume

Aqueduct Park – one location where horse racing is held

aquifer – underground layer of water; one lies under the Pine Barrens

Arthur, Chester A. – twenty-first President of the United States

aviator – someone who flies planes

baleen whale – a type of whale that has long, horny sheets of whalebone instead of teeth

barrier beach – a strip of land separating the mainland from the ocean

Battle of Long Island – an important Revolutionary War battle fought in Brooklyn Heights in 1776

bay – a body of water connected to an ocean and partly enclosed by land

Belmont Park – one location where horse racing is held

biology – the study of living things

Block, Adrian – the first explorer to sail completely around Long Island

blue-collar workers – people who work in non-office type jobs

Board of Elections – holds and supervises elections

Board of Trustees – group that helps the mayor run the government

Boston Tea Party – an uprising against the British tea tax conducted in Boston Harbor in 1773

Brewster, Caleb – a farmer who became a spy

Brookhaven National Laboratory – an atomic power research center

Brooklyn Bridge – built in 1883 joining Brooklyn and Manhattan

Brooklyn Heights – area that overlooks New York Harbor and was the site of one of the first Revolutionary War battles

budget – a plan that shows how a town's tax money will be spent

charter – a legal paper that grants ownership

City Council – elected officials who assist the mayor of a city

Civil Service Commission – oversees hiring of county employees

Civil War – the armed conflict between the northern and southern states fought between 1861 and 1865

cliff – large rocks often near the water's edge

climate – the kind of weather a place has over a period of time

Cold Spring Harbor Laboratory – an internationally known research center for biology

consumer services – shopping and service areas for a community

County Clerk – keeps track of official records, such as property deeds

County Comptroller – watches out for the county's money and okays payments of county money

County Executive – head elected official of county government

County Medical Examiner – investigates suspicious deaths

County Treasurer – handles county's money

cove – a small bay surrounded by hills

Culper Spy Ring – a spy ring on Long Island during the Revolutionary War

current – the flow of water in a certain direction

Curtis, Glenn – a pioneer flier who flew across the Hempstead Plains

Declaration of Independence – an important document written in 1776 that announced America's intent to be free of England

District Attorney – prosecutes criminals

dugout canoe – handmade canoe that was constructed from a tree

Duke's Laws – early British rules for the colonists

Dutch East India Company – Dutch trading company that hired Henry Hudson to find a shorter route to Asia

Dutch West India Company – a Dutch company formed to keep control over Long Island

federal government – makes laws that affect all citizens

Floyd, William – New Yorker who signed the Declaration of Independence

glacier – a large mass of ice

Gold Coast – a series of estates on the North Shore of Long Island

Great Spirit – god worshiped by Native Americans

grist mill – water- or wind-powered mill where grain is ground

Gulf Stream – a warm current of water that flows through the Atlantic Ocean

Hale, Nathan – a spy for George Washington during the Revolutionary War

hamlet – a place like a village but does not have its own government

harbor – a protected body of water where ships can anchor

harpoon – a long spear used to hunt whales

harrow – tool used to make soil smooth

Hudson, Henry – an English explorer who may have discovered Long Island

Ice Age – the very cold period of time thousands of years ago

immigrant – a person who leaves the country where he or she was born to live in a new country

incorporated village – a group of concerned property owners who pay extra taxes for special services

industrial park – an area where many businesses are located together

island – body of land surrounded on all sides by water

King's Highway – early Long Island road going through Brooklyn to Jamaica

Lange Eylandt – Dutch name for Long Island

legislature – one of the three branches of government, the legislature writes the laws

Levittown – a large housing development in Nassau County

Lindbergh, Charles – flew the first non-stop flight across the Atlantic Ocean from New York to Paris

Long Island Rail Road – active system of trains that serves people of Long Island

Long Island Sound – the long body of water that connects the East River to the Atlantic Ocean

Loyalists – colonists who didn't want to break away from British rule

Lunar Excursion Module – a vehicle developed by Grumman and used by American astronauts on the moon

manitous – nature spirits that lived in mountains or rivers

Marine Mammal Protection Act – a law passed to protect whales

mayor – the top elected official of an incorporated village

merge – to combine with another company

Moses, Robert – created state highway system that connected all parts of Long Island

neck – the narrowest part of an island

New Amsterdam – Dutch name for settlement at southern end of Manhattan

New York Islanders – professional ice hockey team that plays on Long Island

Nicolls, Richard – first English governor of New York

nor'easter – a powerful and destructive storm

North Shore – the north part of Long Island, which has many hills and curves

offshore whaling – a way of hunting whales far out to sea

onshore whaling – a method of hunting whales near the shore

Patriots – colonists who wanted to break away from British rule

Paumanok – what Algonquins called Long Island; it means "land of tribute"

peninsula – a piece of land that is surrounded on three sides by water

petition – a request for something signed by a group of voters

Pine Barrens – low growing area of pine trees that retain water

Planning Commission – recommends changes for Long Island growth

preserve – to smoke or dry meat and fruit so it will last a long time

Quakers – a religious group who thought that slavery was wrong

Raynham Hall – Oyster Bay home of the spy Robert Townsend

redcoats – nickname for British soldiers

reservation – area set aside by the government for Native Americans

retail trade – selling goods to the general public

retreat – backing down during a battle and moving backwards

Roebling, John A. – engineer who designed the Brooklyn Bridge

Roosevelt, Theodore – the twenty-sixth President of the United States, who had a home on Long Island

Sachem – a leader of an Algonquin family group

Sagamore Hill – former home of Theodore Roosevelt, located in Oyster Bay

saltbox house – a type of house English colonists lived in

Saratoga – aircraft carrier built in the Brooklyn Navy Yard

sanctuary – a place where animals and birds live and are protected

sand dunes – windswept hills of sand

scrimshaw – carving on whales' teeth

scythe – a heavy tool used for cutting

seawan – another name for wampum, a string of shells used for trading

Second Continental Congress – a meeting of 56 colonists in Philadelphia in 1776

Sheep Parting Day – a colonial holiday

shoreline – the land along the sea

sign language – a silent way of communicating

Social Services – an agency that helps needy people

South Shore – the south part of Long Island, which is very flat and straight

Stamp Act – a British tax on the colonists issued in 1765

state government – makes laws for the state

Strong, Nancy – spy who would give signals to whalebaots with her laundry line

Stuyvesant, Peter – Dutch governor of New Amsterdam from 1647 to 1664

suburb – large area outside a city where many people live

Sunsquaw – a woman Sachem

Tackapausha – a Grand Sachem of the early 1600s who was head of the Massapequa on western Long Island

tax rate – the level at which different people pay taxes

Tech Island – a nickname for Long Island because of the businesses there

toll – money that must be paid in order to use highways and bridges

topsoil – top layer of earth

town board – elected officials of town government

Town Supervisor – chairperson of the town board

turnpike – a road that charges a toll or fee

Verrazano, Giovanni da – sailed into New York Bay in 1524; the Verrazano-Narrows bridge is named after him

Vanderbilt, William K. – wealthy person who paid for the 45-mile highway from Queens to Lake Rononkoma

wampum – string of shells used for trading

whaleboat – a small, light boat used to raid British-occupied Long Island

white-collar workers – people who work in office type jobs

white Pekin ducks – delectable waterfowl introduced to Long Island from China in 1873

Whitman, Walt – a native Long Islander who became a very famous poet

wholesale trade – the sale of goods in large quantities

wigwam – dome-shaped hut made from tree branches

Wyandanch – a great chief of Eastern Long Island in the early 1600s who was known as Sachem of the Montauks